The Actor's

Molière

Volume 1

THE MISER
and
GEORGE DANDIN

in new translations by Albert Bermel

APPLAUSE
THEATRE BOOK PUBLISHERS
211 West 71 Street, New York, NY 10023

Printed in U.S.A.

ISBN O-936839-75-9

Library of Congress Cataloging-in-Publication Data

Molière, 1622–1673.
    The miser and George Dandin.

    (The Actor's Molière ; v. 1)
    Translation of: L'avare and George Dandin.
    1. Molière, 1622–1673—Translations, English.
I. Bermel, Albert. II. Molière, 1622–1673. George
Dandin. 1987. III. Title. IV. Title: George Dandin.
V. Series: Molière, 1622–1673. Actor's Molière ; v. 1.
PQ1825.E5B4   1987   842'.4   87–953
ISBN 0–936839–75–9 (pbk.)

CONTENTS

In memory of my brother Gerald, who lived to the same age as Molière
and loved laughter

GEORGE DANDIN

or The Confounded Husband

(George Dandin, ou Le Mari confondu)

George Dandin, a wealthy farmer of peasant stock
Angélique, his wife
Monsieur de Sotenville, a country gentleman, Angélique's father
Madame de Sotenville, his wife
Clitandre, a courtier from Paris, in love with Angélique
Claudine, Angélique's maidservant
Lubin, a peasant, Clitandre's emissary
Colin, George Dandin's servant

ACT ONE

George Dandin, alone.

GEORGE DANDIN Ah! It's so mortifying to have an upper-class wife. My marriage is a powerful lesson to any peasant who wants to rise above his rank by tying himself, as I've done, to the family of a gentleman. Gentility, as such, is fine, desirable, something you admire, no question about that. But it has too many drawbacks. Stay well out of it! I've learned plenty and it cost me dear. I know what these gentry are after when they recruit the rest of us into their families. They're not interested in us as people. They want to marry our money. I'd have done a lot better, being reasonably well off, to marry into decent, ordinary country folk than to take a wife who thinks she's too good for me, and doesn't like having my name, and acts as if my money isn't enough to pay for the privilege of being her husband. George Dandin, George Dandin, you did the most stupid thing in the world. I've come to hate my house. Every time I enter it I walk into trouble. *(He notices Lubin coming out of his house — aside)* A funny-looking character . . . What the devil's he been up to in my house?

LUBIN *(Aside)* There's a man staring at me.

GEORGE DANDIN *(Aside)* He doesn't know who I am.

LUBIN *(Aside)* He knows something's going on.

GEORGE DANDIN *(Aside)* So! He can hardly bring himself to bow.

LUBIN *(Aside)* I'm afraid he'll tell someone he saw me come out of there.

GEORGE DANDIN Good morning.

LUBIN And to you.

GEORGE DANDIN You're not from these parts, are you?

LUBIN No, I'm here to see the celebrations tomorrow.

GEORGE DANDIN   Excuse me, didn't you just come out of that house?

LUBIN   Shush!

GEORGE DANDIN   What?

LUBIN   Keep it quiet!

GEORGE DANDIN   How come?

LUBIN   Don't ever say you saw me here.

GEORGE DANDIN   Why not?

LUBIN   Because.

GEORGE DANDIN   No, but why not?

LUBIN   Shush now. Someone might be listening.

GEORGE DANDIN   Not a soul.

LUBIN   I just spoke to the lady of the house — a message from a certain gentleman who's sweet on her. Nobody must know about it, you follow?

GEORGE DANDIN   So far.

LUBIN   That's why not. I was told to take care nobody sees me, so I'm asking you not to say a word.

GEORGE DANDIN   I don't need to.

LUBIN   I'm going to keep it secret, like I was told to.

GEORGE DANDIN   That makes sense.

LUBIN   They say the husband's jealous. He doesn't want anybody making love to his wife. He'd kick up a hell of a fuss if he heard about it. Get me?

GEORGE DANDIN   Only too well.

LUBIN   He mustn't know a thing.

GEORGE DANDIN   Why should he?

LUBIN   We'd like to put one over on him, but quietly. You follow?

GEORGE DANDIN   All the way.

LUBIN   If you say you saw me coming out of his house you'll wreck the whole plan, get it?

GEORGE DANDIN   You bet. Ah, what's his name, the one who sent you?

LUBIN   He's our local, you know, big man. Monsieur le Vicomte of something . . . Damn me, I can never remember how the hell they say that name. Monsieur Clee . . . Clit . . . Cleeton . . . I forget.

GEORGE DANDIN   The young nobleman, the one who lives. . . ?

LUBIN   Yes, over by those trees.

GEORGE DANDIN   *(Aside)* So it's the fop who just took a house practically on top of mine. I suspected something, having him that close.

LUBIN   The nicest man you ever met. Gave me three gold pieces just to tell the lady he's in love with her and very much hopes to have the honor of speaking with her. Not a very tiring job, is it, for so much pay? I usually earn about a tenth of that for a whole day's work.

GEORGE DANDIN   And you passed on the message?

LUBIN   Sure did. I came across a servant in there called Claudine. She saw right away what I was after and let me talk to her mistress.

GEORGE DANDIN   *(Aside)* A servant? A whoremonger!

LUBIN   She's a real winner, that Claudine. I've fallen for her. It'll be on her own head if we don't get married.

GEORGE DANDIN   But what did the mistress reply?

LUBIN   She told me to tell him . . . Wait, I don't know if I remember it all . . . She's most grateful for his attentions, but her husband's a monster. None of this must leak out. They'll have to think up some way to meet and talk.

GEORGE DANDIN   *(Aside)* A wife? A tart!

LUBIN   This'll be a laugh. The husband won't know a thing about the arrangement, see? That's what's so great about it. Being jealous won't do him a bit of good, will it?

GEORGE DANDIN   Not much.

LUBIN   So long. Sealed lips, get me? A secret! The husband mustn't find out.

GEORGE DANDIN   He won't from me.

LUBIN   And I'll act like I know nothing. I'm a smart, sly one, and nobody'll guess I'm involved. *(Exit.)*

GEORGE DANDIN   Well, George Dandin, you see how your wife treats you. That's what comes of wanting to marry a lady. She uses you any way she pleases and you can't get back at her. Your hands are tied by class distinctions. When a husband's on a par with his wife he can get as mad as he likes. If she was a peasant girl you'd have every right to thrash her with your heaviest stick. But no, you wanted to move up among the gentry. You weren't satisfied to be master in your own house. Ah, my heart's bursting. I could flog my own hide. The gall of her — to listen to the advances of some dandy from Paris and then promise to meet him in secret! I can't pass up this opportunity. I'll go right to her father and mother and lodge a complaint. I'll get them to witness the pain and anxiety their daughter's causing me. Here they come; that's lucky.

Enter Monsieur and Madame de Sotenville.

MONSIEUR DE SOTENVILLE   What is it, son-in-law? You look worried.

GEORGE DANDIN   I honestly have reason to be, and —

MADAME DE SOTENVILLE Good-heavens, son-in-law, it's not very civil to forget to bow when you approach somebody.

GEORGE DANDIN Now look, mother-in-law, I have other things on my mind, such as —

MADAME DE SOTENVILLE Again! Is it possible that you know so little about common courtesy, son-in-law? Is there no way to teach you how to conduct yourself when you're with people of quality?

GEORGE DANDIN In what way?

MADAME DE SOTENVILLE Can't you stop being familiar and calling me mother-in-law? Won't you ever learn to address me as madame?

GEORGE DANDIN Good lord, if you call me son-in-law I don't see why I can't call you mother-in-law.

MADAME DE SOTENVILLE There are many reasons. The two things are not the same. Kindly realize that you do not use that expression to a person of my standing. You may be our son-in-law, but there's a chasm between you and us. Remember who you are.

MONSIEUR DE SOTENVILLE That's enough, my love. Let us drop it.

MADAME DE SOTENVILLE Good heavens, Monsieur de Sotenville, you're too easygoing for your own good. You don't know how to insist on the respect people owe you.

MONSIEUR DE SOTENVILLE Pardon me, I do not require any lessons on that score. I've vigorously demonstrated at least twenty times in my life that I'm not a man who will yield up one particle of what is due me. But he doesn't need more than a gentle warning. Now, son-in-law, let us hear what is on your mind.

GEORGE DANDIN I'm going to come right out with it, Monsieur de Sotenville, and tell you that I have strong cause to —

MONSIEUR DE SOTENVILLE One moment, son-in-law. Remember that it's impolite to address people by their names. When we speak to a man of superior rank we call him simply monsieur.

GEORGE DANDIN In that case, Simply Monsieur, and not Monsieur de Sotenville any more, I have to tell you that my wife's been giving me a —

MONSIEUR DE SOTENVILLE Stop there. Another thing to remember: you must not say, "my wife," when you speak of our daughter.

GEORGE DANDIN *(Aside)* I can't take any more of this. *(Aloud)* What? My wife's not my wife?

MADAME DE SOTENVILLE Of course she is. But you're not permitted to call her that. You might have done so if you'd married somebody of your own class.

GEORGE DANDIN *(Aside)* You did it, George Dandin, you let yourself in for this. *(Aloud)* Please, just for a moment, forget the gentility and let me speak the best way I can. *(Aside)* To hell with all that fancy bunk! *(Aloud)* I must tell you I'm unhappy about my marriage.

MONSIEUR DE SOTENVILLE And the reason, my boy?

MADAME DE SOTENVILLE What's this? Unhappy with a liaison from which you derive such great advantages?

GEORGE DANDIN What advantages, madame, since I'm supposed to say "madame?" For you it wasn't a bad bargain. Without me, your affairs were, if I may say so, in pitiful shape. My money plugged up plenty of sizable holes. But what did I get out of it, I ask you, except this longer name and title you imposed on me? Instead of being George Dandin, now I'm Monsieur de la Dandinière.

MONSIEUR DE SOTENVILLE My boy, do you question the benefits of being allied to the house of Sotenville?

MADAME DE SOTENVILLE Also the house of Prudoterie, to which I have the honor of belonging and in which nobility is handed on, so to speak, from mother-womb to mother-womb, so that your children will benefit from that splendid privilege and be born gentry.

GEORGE DANDIN Yes, that's fine, my children will be gentry. But me, if something isn't put right, I'll be a cuckold.

MONSIEUR DE SOTENVILLE Exactly what does that mean?

GEORGE DANDIN It means your daughter isn't behaving the way a wife should. She's doing things that are dishonorable.

MADAME DE SOTENVILLE Stop there! Speak cautiously. My daughter descends from a line too virtuous to commit any act that might blemish the name of honesty. In the house of Prudoterie, thank heaven, there hasn't been one woman for over three hundred years about whom anything can be said.

MONSIEUR DE SOTENVILLE Great God, in the house of Sotenville not one loose lady was ever detected. Even the courage inherited by its men doesn't exceed the chastity of its women.

MADAME DE SOTENVILLE We had a Jacqueline de la Prudoterie who declined to become the mistress of a duke, the governor of our province.

MONSIEUR DE SOTENVILLE There was a Mathurine de Sotenville who refused twenty thousand crowns from one of the king's favorites when he asked for nothing more than the honor of speaking to her.

GEORGE DANDIN Well, your daughter isn't that particular. Since she lives with me, she's more sociable.

MONSIEUR DE SOTENVILLE Explain yourself, my boy. We're not people who will defend her if she does wrong. In fact, her mother and I will be the first to make sure that you're treated justly.

MADAME DE SOTENVILLE We won't stand for any laxity in matters of honor. We brought her up with absolute strictness.

GEORGE DANDIN All I can say is that there's a court hanger-on in the neighborhood; you've seen him; he's in love with her; he's making advances right under my nose; and she's very receptive.

MADAME DE SOTENVILLE God on high! I'd strangle her with these hands if she wavered from her mother's standards.

MONSIEUR DE SOTENVILLE By the Almighty! I'd run this sword through her body, hers and the man's, if she blighted her honor.

GEORGE DANDIN   I've told you what's going on. That's my complaint and I must ask for satisfaction.

MONSIEUR DE SOTENVILLE   Don't upset yourself. I'll see you receive it from both of them. I'm the man to put a stop to whatever may have taken place. Are you certain about what you've told us?

GEORGE DANDIN   Positive.

MONSIEUR DE SOTENVILLE   Be sure you are. These are ticklish matters between two gentlemen. One dare not make a hasty move.

GEORGE DANDIN   Once more: everything I've told you is true.

MONSIEUR DE SOTENVILLE   My love, you run along and talk to your daughter about this while I go with my son-in-law to have a word with the man in question.

MADAME DE SOTENVILLE   Is it possible, my pet, that she could so forget herself? You know the impeccable example I've set her.

MONSIEUR DE SOTENVILLE   We'll soon clear this business up. *(Exit Madame de Sotenville.)* Follow me, my boy, and don't fret. You shall see what we're made of when some outsider threatens a member of our family.

GEORGE DANDIN   He's coming this way now.

Enter Clitandre.

MONSIEUR DE SOTENVILLE   Monsieur, am I known to you?

CLITANDRE   I don't believe so, monsieur.

MONSIEUR DE SOTENVILLE   I am the Baron de Sotenville.

CLITANDRE   Charmed.

MONSIEUR DE SOTENVILLE   My name is known in court circles. In my younger days I had the honor of being among the first at the king's assembly of nobles.

CLITANDRE   My congratulations.

MONSIEUR DE SOTENVILLE My father, Monsieur Jean-Gilles de Sotenville, personally took part in the glorious siege of Montauban, forty-seven years ago, and helped wipe out the treacherous Calvinists.

CLITANDRE My warmest compliments.

MONSIEUR DE SOTENVILLE And I have one ancestor, Bertrand de Sotenville, who was so highly thought of in his time that he received permission to sell his entire property and join the Crusades.

CLITANDRE Astonishing. But believable.

MONSIEUR DE SOTENVILLE Monsieur, it has been reported to me that you love and are wooing a young lady, my daughter. I speak on her behalf and also for this man you see here who has the honor to be my son-in-law.

CLITANDRE Who? I?

MONSIEUR DE SOTENVILLE Yes. I'm grateful for this chance to speak to you and invite your explanation.

CLITANDRE It's a slander. Inexplicable! Who told you this, monsieur?

MONSIEUR DE SOTENVILLE Somebody who insists that it is true.

CLITANDRE This somebody is lying. I am a man of honor. Do you think me capable of such base conduct, monsieur? I, in love with a young and lovely lady who has the honor to be the daughter of Monsieur le baron de Sotenville! I have too much respect for you, and I am your obedient servant. Whoever told you that tale is a fool and an outright, unabashed liar.

MONSIEUR DE SOTENVILLE All right, son-in-law.

GEORGE DANDIN What?

CLITANDRE And a worthless mischief maker!

MONSIEUR DE SOTENVILLE Answer him.

GEORGE DANDIN You answer him.

CLITANDRE   If I knew who he is I'd let him experience my sword in his stomach while you watched.

MONSIEUR DE SOTENVILLE   Back up your complaint.

GEORGE DANDIN   It's already backed up. Like a dam. It's the truth.

CLITANDRE   Is it your son-in-law, monsieur, who. . . ?

MONSIEUR DE SOTENVILLE   Yes, he brought it to my attention.

CLITANDRE   He can certainly be thankful for the advantage he has in being allied with you. If it weren't for that, I'd teach him a painful lesson for spreading such stories about a gentleman like myself.

Enter Madame de Sotenville, Angélique, and Claudine.

MADAME DE SOTENVILLE   I've brought my daughter here to clear up this matter. Jealousy is an ugly business.

CLITANDRE   Was it you, madame, who told your husband I love you?

ANGELIQUE   I? How could I have told him? Is that how it is? I'd like to see what would happen if you were really in love with me. Pretend, will you, please? You'll find out what kind of person I am. I dare you. Make the attempt. Practice all the usual lovers' stratagems. Send me messages for the fun of it. Write me secret love notes. Declare your passion when my husband is absent or when I'm out of the house. Just try, and I promise you'll get the response you deserve.

CLITANDRE   Hold on, madame. It's not necessary to give me detailed instructions and to work up such indignation. Who told you I had any notion of loving you?

ANGELIQUE   How do I know, from the nonsense I've heard here?

CLITANDRE   They may say what they like, but you know whether I've spoken to you about love when I've met you.

ANGELIQUE   If you did you'd get a warm welcome.

CLITANDRE I swear you have nothing to fear from me. I'd never offend a reputable lady. I have too much respect for you and for your esteemed parents to dream of falling in love with you.

MADAME DE SOTENVILLE You see, son-in-law?

MONSIEUR DE SOTENVILLE Now my boy, you have no further cause for suspicion. What do you say to that?

GEORGE DANDIN I say it's hokum, start to finish. I know what I know. And I must speak out. She just received a message from him.

ANGELIQUE I received a message?

CLITANDRE I sent a message?

ANGELIQUE Claudine.

CLITANDRE Is that true?

CLAUDINE On my word, it's an out-and-out falsehood.

GEORGE DANDIN Quiet, you troublemaker! I know what your game is. You're the one who let the messenger in.

CLAUDINE I did?

GEORGE DANDIN Yes, you. You! Syrup wouldn't melt in your mouth.

CLAUDINE Oh, dear, the world's so full of wickedness these days. Imagine accusing me when I don't have a glimmer of an idea what he's talking about.

GEORGE DANDIN That's enough, you tricky slut. You can play the innocent, but I got your number long ago, you two-face.

CLAUDINE Madame is it —?

GEORGE DANDIN Enough, I said. You may end up paying the penalty for everybody because you don't have a father who's a gentleman.

ANGELIQUE   This is such a wild allegation, and it wounds me so
deeply, that I haven't the strength to argue about it. It's especially
horrible to be blamed by a husband when I've done not one thing to
him I shouldn't have. All I'm guilty of is having been too
accommodating to him.

CLAUDINE   So she is.

ANGELIQUE   This is my reward for giving him too much. I wish to
heaven I could endure advances from somebody, as he says I do,
then there would be less reason to pity me. Good-by. I must go. I
can't face any more affronts of this kind.   *(Exit.)*

MADAME DE SOTENVILLE   There, son-in-law! You don't deserve
the virtuous wife we gave you.

CLAUDINE   He deserves to have her do what he says she did. If I
was in her shoes, I wouldn't hesitate.   *(To Clitandre)*   Yes,
monsieur, punish him by falling in love with my mistress. Go
ahead, I'm telling you to. It'll be tit for tat. I offer to help you now
he's accused me of already doing so.   *(Exit.)*

MONSIEUR DE SOTENVILLE   You asked for all this, my boy. Your
conduct sets everyone against you.

MADAME DE SOTENVILLE   Yes, learn how to treat a wellborn
young lady, and take care from now on to avoid any similar
blunders.   *(Exit.)*

GEORGE DANDIN   *(Aside)*   This tears me open: to be in the wrong
when I'm right.

CLITANDRE   Monsieur de Sotenville, You can see I've been
slandered. You're a man who understands the fine points of
gentlemanly etiquette, and I ask satisfaction from you for the injury
I've suffered.

MONSIEUR DE SOTENVILLE   That's fair. It's also correct
procedure. Come, my boy, give the gentleman satisfaction.

GEORGE DANDIN   Satisfaction?

MONSIEUR DE SOTENVILLE   Yes, according to the rules of honor,
because you made a false accusation.

GEORGE DANDIN I can't agree about the falseness of the accusation. I have my own opinion about that.

MONSIEUR DE SOTENVILLE Your opinion doesn't count. Whatever you still think, he's acquitted himself. That requires satisfaction because nobody has the right to hold a man responsible for an action he disavows.

GEORGE DANDIN So then, if I find him in bed with my wife and he disavows it, he isn't responsible?

MONSIEUR DE SOTENVILLE No more quibbling. Apologize to him. I'll dictate the words.

GEORGE DANDIN I'm to apologize, after he ... !

MONSIEUR DE SOTENVILLE Come on, I tell you. We've settled all this. You don't have to be afraid of overdoing the apology when you have me advising you.

GEORGE DANDIN I can't!

MONSIEUR DE SOTENVILLE Great God, son-in-law, don't get my dander up or I'll go over to his side. Now — put yourself in my charge.

GEORGE DANDIN Ah, George Dandin!

MONSIEUR DE SOTENVILLE First: your hat in your hand. Monsieur is a gentleman and you're not.

GEORGE DANDIN *(Aside)* I'm on fire!

MONSIEUR DE SOTENVILLE Repeat after me: Monsieur...

GEORGE DANDIN "Monsieur..."

MONSIEUR DE SOTENVILLE I ask your pardon. *(George Dandin hesitates.)* Out with it!

GEORGE DANDIN "I ask your pardon. Out with it."

MONSIEUR DE SOTENVILLE For thinking ill of you...

GEORGE DANDIN   "For thinking ill of you . . ."

MONSIEUR DE SOTENVILLE   When I did not have the honor of
knowing you . . .

GEORGE DANDIN   "When I did not have the honor of knowing
you . . ."

MONSIEUR DE SOTENVILLE   And I beg you to believe . . .

GEORGE DANDIN   "And I beg you to believe . . ."

MONSIEUR DE SOTENVILLE   That I am your servant.

GEORGE DANDIN   You want to make me the servant of a man who
wants to make me a cuckold?

MONSIEUR DE SOTENVILLE   *(Threatening him)* Ha!

CLITANDRE   That is ample, monsieur.

MONSIEUR DE SOTENVILLE   No, I want him to round it off
properly. Everything must go according to form. That I am your
servant . . .

GEORGE DANDIN   "That I am your servant."

CLITANDRE   I am yours too, monsieur, with all my heart. I'll pay
no further heed to what has happened. Good day to you, Monsieur
le Baron de Sotenville. I am sorry for the inconvenience you've
had.

MONSIEUR DE SOTENVILLE   Nothing at all. Any time you feel like
shooting a brace of hare I'll be delighted to entertain you.

CLITANDRE   You are too kind. *(Exit.)*

MONSIEUR DE SOTENVILLE   There, my boy, that's how these
things are handled. Good-by. Remember, you've been accepted
into a family that will back you to the hilt and never allow you to be
insulted. *(Exit.)*

GEORGE DANDIN   *(Alone)*   Oh, if only I . . . But you wanted it,
you wanted it, George Dandin, you wanted it. You asked for it and

you got what you asked for. It serves you right. Now the only answer is to open her parents' eyes. Maybe I'll find some way to succeed. Maybe.

ACT TWO

Claudine and Lubin.

CLAUDINE Yes, I guessed it came from you. Somebody you told reported it to the master.

LUBIN Here's the truth. I dropped a word or two in passing to a man here so he wouldn't say he saw me leave the house. People around here must tattle a lot.

CLAUDINE This Monsieur le Vicomte sure knows how to choose his servants, taking you on as his go-between! He got the pick of the bunch.

LUBIN Never mind, next time I'll be smarter. I'll play it very tight-lipped.

CLAUDINE About time.

LUBIN Let's not get into that now. Listen.

CLAUDINE To what?

LUBIN Turn your face a bit more toward me.

CLAUDINE Oh? Why?

LUBIN Claudine!

CLAUDINE What?

LUBIN Don't you see what I'm getting at?

CLAUDINE No.

LUBIN Hell, I love you.

CLAUDINE For real?

LUBIN So help me God.

CLAUDINE I'm thrilled.

LUBIN When I look at you I feel my heart go bump, thump, jump.

CLAUDINE You've just made my day.

LUBIN What do you do to be so pretty?

CLAUDINE The same as everyone else.

LUBIN Look, no use beating around the bush. If you like, be my wife, I'll be your husband, and the two of us'll be husband and wife.

CLAUDINE Maybe you'll be jealous like the master.

LUBIN Not me.

CLAUDINE I hate possessive husbands. I want mine to be so trusting and so sure of my love that he wouldn't have a single doubt if he saw me surrounded by thirty men.

LUBIN That's how I'll be.

CLAUDINE It's dumb to distrust a wife and torment her. Doesn't do any good. It gives her naughty ideas. Husbands who make trouble like that have themselves to thank for what they turn into.

LUBIN Yes, I'll give you your freedom. I'll let you do anything you like.

CLAUDINE That's it, you must, then you won't be deceived. When a husband gives us our own way we don't take any more freedom than we should. It's like having someone who opens his purse to us and says, "Help yourself." We'll treat him fair and square and be satisfied with what's reasonable. But the ones who drive us crazy with their meanness and nasty suspicious ideas — we do our best to keep them worried. We don't show them any mercy.

LUBIN Listen, I'll be the type who opens his purse. All you have to do is marry me. Isn't that simple?

CLAUDINE We'll see.

LUBIN Come closer then, Claudine.

CLAUDINE What for?

LUBIN Just, you know, pull in tight.

CLAUDINE Take it easy. I don't like men with wandering hands.

LUBIN Only a little spot of affection.

CLAUDINE Leave me alone, I said. I don't understand these jokes.

LUBIN Claudine!

CLAUDINE Ow! *(She attacks him back.)*

LUBIN Why are you so rough on me? I'm surprised at you. It's not right to give people the cold shoulder. Aren't you ashamed? All those good looks and you won't let a man have a touch. Selfish!

CLAUDINE I'll give you a touch on the snoot.

LUBIN Oh you wild one, you savage! Cruel, heartless.

CLAUDINE You're too forward.

LUBIN Would it hurt you to let me have a little squeeze?

CLAUDINE Be patient.

LUBIN One tiny kiss then, before the marriage. On account.

CLAUDINE Nothing doing.

LUBIN Claudine, please! An advance! A loan!

CLAUDINE Not a hope. I've been that route before. Good-by. Go tell Monsieur le Vicomte I'll be sure to deliver his note.

LUBIN Good-by, beautiful slave-driver.

CLAUDINE Don't turn my head.

LUBIN Good-by, rock, boulder, flint, granite, dagger, sword, and everything that's hardest and sharpest. *(Exit.)*

CLAUDINE Insipid drip. I'll go in and give the mistress this. Oh, here she comes. But her husband is with her. I'll wait. *(Exit.)*

Enter Angélique, George Dandin, and separately, Clitandre, who stands behind George Dandin.

GEORGE DANDIN Oh no, you don't slip one over on me that easily. I'm certain the report I received is the truth. My eyes are sharper than you think, and they were not dazzled by your performance.

CLITANDRE *(Aside)* She's there! But the husband's with her.

GEORGE DANDIN I can see that what I was told is true, behind all those faces you're making. *(She is greeting Clitandre.)* And also your contempt for our marriage vows. *(Angélique and Clitandre exchange bows.)* You can skip the bowing. That's not the sort of respect I look for. There's no need to be sarcastic.

ANGELIQUE Sarcastic? Me? Nothing of the sort.

GEORGE DANDIN I know what you think, and I realize ... *(Another exchange of bows.)* Again? Enough of this mockery. I'm aware that you look down on me because of your class. The respect I look for has nothing to do with me as a person. I'm referring to the sacred ties of marriage. *(Angélique shrugs as a sign to Clitandre.)* What are you shrugging your shoulders for? I'm not talking rubbish.

ANGELIQUE I wouldn't dream of shrugging my shoulders to you.

GEORGE DANDIN I saw you clearly. I say again: marriage is a bond that demands all our respect, and you're immoral to abuse it the way you do. *(Angélique shakes her head and smiles.)* Yes, immoral. How come you're shaking your head and grinning at me.

ANGELIQUE Me? I don't know what you mean.

GEORGE DANDIN I know what I mean, all too well. You despise me. I may not be highborn, but my family has a good name. The Dandins always --

Clitandre moves to behind Angélique without being spotted by George Dandin, and whispers to her.

CLITANDRE A brief chat, when you can?

GEORGE DANDIN What was that?

ANGELIQUE I didn't say a word.

George Dandin goes around his wife. Clitandre bows to him and goes off.

GEORGE DANDIN It was that character who hangs around you.

ANGELIQUE Well, is it my fault? What do you expect me to do about it?

GEORGE DANDIN I expect you to behave like a wife who tries to please nobody but her husband. Whatever people say, these gallant types don't persist unless they get some encouragement. A certain sweet manner that says, "I'm available" draws them the way honey does flies. Decent women have a haughty air that scares them off.

ANGELIQUE Why should I scare them off? It doesn't shock me if men find me attractive. I like it.

GEORGE DANDIN Oh yes? And what part is your husband to play while this flirting goes on?

ANGELIQUE The part of a man who honestly appreciates seeing his wife admired.

GEORGE DANDIN Not for me. The Dandins do things differently.

ANGELIQUE The Dandins can do whatever they please. I don't intend to give up the world and bury myself alive with my husband. What? Because men take it into their heads to marry us, does everything else come to an end? Do we cut off our connections with every living soul? This tyranny of husbands is outrageous.

They want us dead to all diversions, alive for them only. Very kind of them. I refuse to die so young.

GEORGE DANDIN   Is this how you honor your public promise?

ANGELIQUE   I didn't give it willingly. You snatched it from me. Did you ask me beforehand if I wanted to marry you? You spoke to my father and mother only. Properly speaking, they're the ones you married, and that's why it'll always make sense for you to go griping to them when you feel hard done by. I never advised you to marry me, much less consented. You took me without asking about my feelings, and I don't see now why I need submit to your wishes like a slave. If you don't mind, I'd like to make the most of the few happy years of youth I still have, to take advantage of this precious, carefree age, see something of fine society, and enjoy listening to pretty compliments. This is your punishment, so face up to it. And thank your stars I'm not capable of doing anything worse.

GEORGE DANDIN   Is that your attitude? Well, as your husband, I say I won't have it.

ANGELIQUE   I'm your wife, and I say I will have it.

GEORGE DANDIN   *(Aside)* I'd like to smash her face to a pulp so that it'll never again charm those mealy-mouthed parasites. Oh, come on, George Dandin, better leave before you lose control. *(Exit.)*

Re-enter Claudine.

CLAUDINE   He had me fidgeting, madame, waiting for him to leave. Here's a note from you-know-whom.

ANGELIQUE   Let me see!

CLAUDINE   You don't look unhappy about it.

ANGELIQUE   Oh Claudine, this is such an elegant message! Courtiers are so pleasing in their speech and manners. Not like our provincial hicks.

CLAUDINE   Such as the Dandin tribe?

ANGELIQUE   Stay here. I'll go in and write a reply. *(Exit.)*

CLAUDINE I don't have to advise her to make it tempting. But he's here...

(*Enter Clitandre and Lubin.*) Well, monsieur, you found yourself a smart messenger here.

CLITANDRE I didn't dare send one of my own people. But Claudine, my dear, I must give you something for the generous things you've done for me.

CLAUDINE Not necessary, monsieur. No, monsieur, you don't have to bother. I help you because you deserve it, and I also feel good about you.

CLITANDRE *(Handing her money)* Thank you.

LUBIN Now we're going to be married, let me take it and add it to mine.

CLAUDINE I'll hold it for you, together with the kiss.

CLITANDRE Did you give my note to your lovely mistress?

CLAUDINE Yes. She's gone in to write a reply.

CLITANDRE Isn't there any way I can speak to her?

CLAUDINE Sure, I'll let you have a word with her. Come with me.

CLITANDRE Won't she object? Isn't it risky?

CLAUDINE No, no, her husband's not in. Anyway, she watches out less for him than for her father and mother. As long as they're on her side she has nothing to be scared of.

CLITANDRE Lead the way.

Exeunt Claudine and Clitandre.

LUBIN Holy mo, what a clever wife I'm going to have! She has brains enough for four.

Enter George Dandin.

GEORGE DANDIN   *(Aside)* Here's my informant from before. I wish to God I could persuade him to testify before her disbelieving mother and father.

LUBIN   So it's you, bigmouth, after I gave you orders not to blow the story and you swore you wouldn't. Can't hold on to a secret, hey, even when it's a secret that's private and confidential?

GEORGE DANDIN   You mean me?

LUBIN   Who else? You went and told the husband everything. He made a row about it, and you're to blame. I'm glad to know what a long tongue you have. That taught me something, that did.

GEORGE DANDIN   Listen, my dear fellow...

LUBIN   If you hadn't let it out I'd have put you wise to what's going on. Now, for your punishment, I won't tell you one thing.

GEORGE DANDIN   But what *is* going on?

LUBIN   Silence, that's all you'll get from me. Not one word. Not another taste. I'll leave you with your mouth watering.

GEORGE DANDIN   Wait a second.

LUBIN   No.

GEORGE DANDIN   Let me just mention —

LUBIN   Will I hell! You want to worm the information out of me.

GEORGE DANDIN   That's not it.

LUBIN   You take me for a dope. But I see what you're after.

GEORGE DANDIN   It's something else. Listen.

LUBIN   Forget it. You'd like me to tell you how Monsieur le Vicomte gave Claudine some money and she took him indoors to see her mistress. But you don't get it out of me. I'm not that stupid.

GEORGE DANDIN   Please.

LUBIN Never.

GEORGE DANDIN I'll give you —

LUBIN A stiff finger! *(Exit.)*

GEORGE DANDIN I'll never get that simpleton to testify. But this new information he dropped can serve the same purpose. If her admirer's in the house, that's all I need to make her mother and father see I was right and convince them that she's openly fickle. The trouble is, I don't know how to capitalize on the information. If I walk into the house he'll run away. Even if I watch them betraying me, the old couple won't believe me; they'll say it's all in my imagination. If, on the other hand, I go and bring my in-laws without being sure he's inside, it'll be the same story as before. I'll land in the same mess as I did this morning. Maybe I can quietly check whether he's still there. *(He peers through the keyhole.)* Yes! No question about it. I saw him. Now I can cramp their style and put a stop to the affair, because here come the members of the jury. *(Enter Monsieur and Madame de Sotenville.)* You wouldn't believe me before, would you? Your daughter won out. But this time I have proof of how she treats me. Thank God, my disgrace is now so plain you won't have any more doubts.

MONSIEUR DE SOTENVILLE What is it, my boy? Harping on that again?

GEORGE DANDIN I certainly am, and I never had better reason.

MADAME DE SOTENVILLE You're still dinning that into everybody's head?

GEORGE DANDIN Yes, madame, because someone's doing a lot worse to mine.

MONSIEUR DE SOTENVILLE Aren't you tired of making a nuisance of yourself?

GEORGE DANDIN I'm tired of being made a laughingstock.

MADAME DE SOTENVILLE Won't you ever give up these fantasies?

GEORGE DANDIN Madame, I'd rather give up a wife who disgraces me.

MADAME DE SOTENVILLE   Watch your language, son-in-law.

MONSIEUR DE SOTENVILLE   Choose expressions that are less offensive.

GEORGE DANDIN   Politeness is for those who feel up to it.

MADAME DE SOTENVILLE   Remember: you're married to a lady.

GEORGE DANDIN   I'll never allow myself to forget it.

MADAME DE SOTENVILLE   Then speak of her with more respect.

GEORGE DANDIN   Why doesn't she treat me with more respect? Because she's a lady, does it mean she can do what she likes to me and I mustn't let out a murmur?

MONSIEUR DE SOTENVILLE   What are you getting at? Are you saying something? Didn't you see this morning how she denied knowing the man you told me about?

GEORGE DANDIN   Yes, but wouldn't you be up in arms too if I told you he's with her now?

MADAME DE SOTENVILLE   With my virtuous daughter?

GEORGE DANDIN   There, yes, in my house.

MONSIEUR DE SOTENVILLE   Inside your house?

GEORGE DANDIN   My house, yes, mine.

MADAME DE SOTENVILLE   If that's so, we'll certainly take your side against her.

MONSIEUR DE SOTENVILLE   Indeed, yes. Our reputation is more precious to us than anything else. If you're telling the truth, we'll expel her from our family and leave her to face your wrath.

GEORGE DANDIN   Follow me.

MADAME DE SOTENVILLE   Just be certain you're not mistaken.

MONSIEUR DE SOTENVILLE   As you were this morning.

GEORGE DANDIN You'll soon see. There! Was I lying?

Angélique and Clitandre appear in the doorway. Claudine stands outside by the door.

ANGELIQUE Good-by. I'm nervous: someone may surprise you here. I must take all precautions.

CLITANDRE Promise then, madame, that I'll speak to you tonight.

ANGELIQUE I'll do my best.

GEORGE DANDIN *(To the De Sotenvilles)* Creep closer, behind them. Try not to let them see us.

CLAUDINE Madame! We're done for. Your father and mother are back there with your husband.

CLITANDRE Oh God!

ANGELIQUE Pretend you haven't seen anything. Leave this to me. *(Noisily)* What! You dare visit my home after what happened earlier? This is how you go back on your word. I was told you were in love with me and might make advances. I openly expressed my indignation. You saw it in front of my family. You coolly denied the whole thing, and swore you had no thought of offending me. Then, the same day, you have the audacity to enter my house and tell me you love me to soften me up for your infamous proposals! As if I'm a wife who'd shatter the vows I made to my husband or endanger the virtue my parents instilled in me! If my father knew, he'd teach you to play these frivolous games. But a decent woman doesn't create scandal. I have no desire to distress him. I'm going to show you that even though I'm a woman, I'm bold enough to answer back when I'm affronted. Your conduct is not worthy of a gentleman and I won't treat you like one.

She seizes a stick handed to her by Claudine and beats her husband, instead of Clitandre, who has moved out of the way.

CLITANDRE Ow, ow, ow, ow, ow! Stop! *(Exit.)*

CLAUDINE Harder, madame, he asked for it.

ANGELIQUE *(Calling after Clitandre)* If there's anything else on your mind, I have another answer ready.

CLAUDINE *(Calling)* Choose more suitable playmates.

ANGELIQUE Oh father, are you here?

MONSIEUR DE SOTENVILLE Yes, my girl. And I see that when it comes to good sense and courage, you prove yourself a true child of the Sotenvilles. Come, let me embrace you.

MADAME DE SOTENVILLE Embrace me too, darling. Look, I'm weeping for joy. When you did that just now I recognized my own flesh and blood.

MONSIEUR DE SOTENVILLE And how delighted you must be, my boy! This incident will have cheered you up immensely. You had good cause for alarm, but now your suspicions have been beautifully dispelled.

MADAME DE SOTENVILLE Yes, son-in-law, you must be the happiest man alive.

CLAUDINE Should be.   That's some wife for you. You don't value her the way you should. You ought to kiss the ground she walks on.

GEORGE DANDIN *(Aside)* Treacherous slut!

MONSIEUR DE SOTENVILLE What's wrong with you, my boy? Why don't you say a word of thanks to your wife for her loyalty?

ANGELIQUE No, no, father. That's not necessary. He owes me nothing for what he saw. I did it out of self-respect.

MONSIEUR DE SOTENVILLE Where are you going?

ANGELIQUE Indoors. I don't want to have to accept his thanks. *(Exit.)*

CLAUDINE She's right to be upset. A wife like that ought to be worshiped. You don't treat her as graciously as you should. *(Exit.)*

GEORGE DANDIN *(Aside)* Vixen! Slop! Bawd!

MONSIEUR DE SOTENVILLE   Still a little sore after this morning?
Once you've given her a few caresses you'll be over it. Good-by,
my boy. You have nothing more to grumble about. Go and make
up. Beg her to forgive you for losing control of yourself.

MADAME DE SOTENVILLE   You must realize she's a lady schooled
in virtue; she's not used to being suspected of wrongdoing. Good-
by. I'm so glad your misunderstanding is settled. I know you feel
blissful about her conduct.

Exeunt Monsieur and Madame de Sotenville.

GEORGE DANDIN   I'm not saying a word. Speaking won't do me
any good. Nobody ever had a worse plight than mine. Yes, I
marvel at my misfortune. And at my evil wife's cunning as she
makes herself look right and me wrong. Will I always come out the
loser? always find appearances twisted against me? never manage
to turn the tables? I'm so miserable. The loser never laughs. Oh
God, help me! Grant me the blessing of letting others see how
dishonored I am!

ACT THREE

Clitandre and Lubin.

CLITANDRE   The night's wearing on. I'm afraid we're late. I can't
see where I'm going. Lubin!

LUBIN   Monsieur?

CLITANDRE   Is it this way?

LUBIN   I think so. Goddam, what a stupid night to make itself so
dark.

CLITANDRE   It certainly went too far. But if it prevents us from
seeing, it also prevents us from being seen.

LUBIN   You're right. The night's not so wrong. I'd like to ask,
monsieur, you being a learned man, why it's not day at night.

CLITANDRE   That's a big question, a hard one. You're hungry for knowledge, Lubin.

LUBIN   I am. If I studied, I'd go on to think of things nobody else ever thought of.

CLITANDRE   I believe that. You give the impression of having a subtle and penetrating intellect.

LUBIN   It's true. Look, I can explain Latin, though I never learned any. The other day when I saw the word *collegium* over a high doorway, I guessed it meant colleague. The people who live there are colleagues, pals.

CLITANDRE   You can read, then?

LUBIN   Oh yes, I can read words, but not whole sentences.

CLITANDRE   We should be close to the house now. *(He claps his hands.)* That's the signal Claudine gave me.

LUBIN   On my oath, that's a girl worth a fortune. I love her with all my heart, most of it.

CLITANDRE   That's why I brought you along. To entertain her.

LUBIN   Monsieur, I'm most —

CLITANDRE   Hush, I hear something.

Enter Angélique and Claudine.

ANGELIQUE   Claudine.

CLAUDINE   Well?

ANGELIQUE   Leave the door open.

CLAUDINE   I did.

CLITANDRE   There they are. Psst!

ANGELIQUE   Psst!

LUBIN Psst!

CLAUDINE Psst!

CLITANDRE *(To Claudine)* Madame!

ANGELIQUE *(To Lubin)* What?

LUBIN *(To Angélique)* Claudine!

CLAUDINE *(To Clitandre)* Yes?

CLITANDRE *(To Claudine)* Oh, madame, I'm so happy . . .

LUBIN *(To Angélique)* Claudine, my dear Claudine . . .

CLAUDINE *(To Clitandre)* Not so fast, monsieur.

ANGELIQUE *(To Lubin)* Lubin, that'll do.

CLITANDRE Is that you, Claudine?

CLAUDINE Yes.

LUBIN Is that you, madame?

ANGELIQUE Yes.

CLAUDINE You grabbed one of us for the other.

LUBIN Can't see a thing in this stinking dark.

ANGELIQUE Is this you, Clitandre?

CLITANDRE Yes, madame.

ANGELIQUE My husband's snoring away. Our chance to talk!

CLITANDRE Let's find a place to sit.

CLAUDINE That's a good thought.

The three of them sit at the rear of the stage.

LUBIN   Claudine!   Where'd you get to?

George Dandin comes from the house with his shirt hanging out.

GEORGE DANDIN   *(Aside)*   I heard my wife come down and I dressed in a hurry to follow her. Where did she get to? Out here?

LUBIN   Claudine, where are you? *(Taking George Dandin for Claudine)* Ah, here you are! We tricked your master beautifully. This is as funny as that clobbering I hear your mistress gave him. She says he's snoring like a demon. He won't dream she's been with Monsieur le Vicomte. Or maybe he will. It's a laugh. What business does he have being jealous of his wife, trying to keep her to himself? He has some nerve. Doesn't he see that Monsieur le Vicomte is doing him an honor? Claudine, you're not saying a word. Come, let's join the others. Give me your precious little handy to kiss. It's so soft. Like nibbling cookies. *(He kisses George Dandin's hand again. Dandin roughly pushes his face away.)* Hey, what's this about? You have such a hard little fisty.

GEORGE DANDIN   Who is this?

LUBIN   Nobody.   *(Exit.)*

GEORGE DANDIN   So this is my harlot wife's latest maneuver. I mustn't waste time. I'll send for her father and mother, and get free of her for good. Hey, Colin, Colin!

COLIN   *(At the window)*   Yes, master?

GEORGE DANDIN   Here, quick, come down.

COLIN   *(Having jumped out of the window)*   I'm here. Couldn't do it quicker.

GEORGE DANDIN   Is this you, over here?

COLIN   Yes, master.

George Dandin goes one way to meet Colin. Colin goes the other way, sits down, falls asleep.

GEORGE DANDIN Speak low. Listen. Run to my in-laws' house and tell them it's urgent they come over here as fast as they can. You hear me? Colin, Colin!

COLIN *(Waking)* Yes, master?

GEORGE DANDIN Where are you?

COLIN Right here.

They cross paths to opposite sides of the stage.

GEORGE DANDIN Thickwit! Bonehead! You're wandering. I told you to go for my in-laws and urge them to come here without delay. Did you hear that? Answer me! Colin, Colin!

COLIN *(On the other side)* Yes, master?

GEORGE DANDIN He's going to drive me mad. Come to where I am. *(They collide.)* Oh, the lout! He crippled me. Where are you? Come nearer so I can wallop you. I think he's avoiding me.

COLIN Sure am.

GEORGE DANDIN Will you come over here?

COLIN Not on your life.

GEORGE DANDIN I said, Come!

COLIN You'll wallop me.

GEORGE DANDIN No, I won't touch you.

COLIN Honest?

GEORGE DANDIN Yes! Come here. Good. Lucky for you I need you. Run to my in-laws' place and beg them to come here as fast as they can. Tell them it's vital. If they make any difficulty because of the time, insist. Make them realize it's desperately important for them to be here, whatever state they're in. You heard me this time?

COLIN Yes, master.

GEORGE DANDIN   Now hurry. And hurry back. *(Exit Colin.)* I'll go into the house while . . . Did I hear someone? Was that my wife? I'd better listen under cover of the darkness.

ANGELIQUE   Goodnight. It's time to go.

CLITANDRE   What? So soon?

ANGELIQUE   We've talked long enough.

CLITANDRE   But madame, how can it be long enough for me to talk to you with so little time to find my words? I'd need days to make you understand my feelings, and I haven't told you a fraction of what I long to say.

ANGELIQUE   I'll hear more some other time.

CLITANDRE   You strike me to the soul when you speak of going. You'll leave me here heartbroken.

ANGELIQUE   It's not as if we won't meet again.

CLITANDRE   Yes, but you're leaving me for a husband. That thought rankles in me. A husband's privileges are cruel blows to a devoted lover.

ANGELIQUE   You can't be silly enough to worry about that. Do you think husbands like him are capable of arousing love? We take them because we can't help ourselves. We're at the mercy of parents who have eyes for nothing but wealth. Luckily we know how to pay these husbands back. We show them no more consideration than they're worth.

GEORGE DANDIN   *(Aside)*   So much for our whorish wives.

CLITANDRE   Yes, I must say the one they dug up for you is hardly equal to the blessing bestowed on him. A match between a lady like you and a boor like him — it's unbelievable!

GEORGE DANDIN   Poor husbands! What a cross you have to bear!

CLITANDRE   You surely deserve a much kinder fate. Heaven didn't create a woman like you to become a peasant's wife.

GEORGE DANDIN *(Aside)* Would to God she was yours! You'd soon talk out of the other side of your mouth. I'm going in. I've had enough.

He enters the house and locks the door.

CLAUDINE Madame, if you have anything bad left to say about your husband, speak fast. It's late.

CLITANDRE Claudine, you're too cruel.

ANGELIQUE But she's right. Let's part now.

CLITANDRE If that's your wish. But please have pity on me for the hours of anguish I'll have to live through.

ANGELIQUE Goodnight.

Exit Clitandre.

LUBIN Claudine, where are you, so I can give you a goodnight?

CLAUDINE Go, go. I'll take it — and return it — from a distance.

Exit Lubin.

ANGELIQUE Don't make a sound as you go in.

CLAUDINE The door's locked!

ANGELIQUE I have the master key.

CLAUDINE Open it gently.

ANGELIQUE It's bolted on the inside. I don't know what we can do.

CLAUDINE Call the boy. He sleeps in there.

ANGELIQUE Colin! Colin! Colin!

GEORGE DANDIN *(Putting his head out of his window)* Colin, Colin? Caught you at it this time, madame, didn't I? Running loose, hey, while I'm asleep? How do you like it out of doors at this hour?

ANGELIQUE   What's wrong with taking a cool breath of night air?

GEORGE DANDIN   Yes, of course, it's the time for coolness. And heat, Madame Strumpet. I know the whole story, this meeting with your fop. I heard the gallant conversation and how you praised me. But my turn is coming. Your father and mother will be convinced at last. They'll see I have a legitimate complaint. I've sent for them. They'll be here any minute.

ANGELIQUE   Oh God!

CLAUDINE   Oh hell!

GEORGE DANDIN   Here's a situation you didn't expect. This time I've come out on top. I have all the evidence I need to take your pride down a few pegs. Up to now you kept making fun of my accusations. You pulled the wool over your parents' eyes, and lied your way out of mischief. It did me no good to see it for myself or talk about it. Your cunning always won out over my honesty. You made yourself appear to be in the right. But at last, thank God, I've foiled you. The truth will come to light.

ANGELIQUE   Please, I beg of you, open the door.

GEORGE DANDIN   Not yet. We must wait for our witnesses. I summoned them and I want them to find you out there at this hour. Until they arrive you can strain your brains, if you feel like it, for a new strategy to get you out of this pickle. Dream up a way to justify your little escapade, some smart move that will blind everybody and make you look blameless — a phony tale about a pilgrimage by night or a friend in labor you went to help.

ANGELIQUE   No, I'm not going to mislead you. I won't defend myself or deny things you already know.

GEORGE DANDIN   That's because you're in a hopeless spot. I can easily pick holes in any of your inventions.

ANGELIQUE   All right, I admit I did wrong and you had cause for your complaints. But I ask you to be generous and not make me face my parents' rage. Hurry, open the door!

GEORGE DANDIN   Kiss my hand.

ANGELIQUE   My own dear husband, I entreat you!

GEORGE DANDIN   Oho, your own dear husband. I'm your dear husband now you realize you're trapped. I'm delighted to hear that. You never thought of tossing bouquets at me before.

ANGELIQUE   Wait! I promise I'll never make you unhappy again, and I'll —

GEORGE DANDIN   Don't waste your breath. I'm determined not to lose this round. It means a lot to me to show you up for what you are.

ANGELIQUE   Please let me say something. I'm asking you to listen for one moment.

GEORGE DANDIN   For one moment. Go ahead.

ANGELIQUE   I'm to blame; it's true. I admit it again. You have every right to feel resentful. I did take the opportunity to slip out while you were asleep, and I did go for a rendez-vous with the person you mentioned. But can't you pardon misdemeanors like these because of my age? Can't you forgive the eagerness of a young woman who has seen nothing and only just begun to meet people? These are liberties it's easy to fall into without meaning to do wrong. They don't amount to anything that —

GEORGE DANDIN   Yes, that's what you keep saying. I've learned not to take these statements on trust.

ANGELIQUE   I'm not trying to excuse myself. I did provoke you. I'm only pleading with you to forget my offense, and I ask your pardon with all my heart. This one time spare me the ordeal of those angry reproaches from my father and mother. If you can be generous and merciful, this kind gesture of yours will win me over. It will touch me to the heart and plant a feeling for you there that my parents' power and the obligations of marriage couldn't awaken. I'm saying that, because of this gesture, I'll give up all flirtations. I'll form no attachments, except to you. Yes, I give you my word that from now on you'll find me a model wife. I'll show you so much affection, so much affection, that it will be all you want or need.

GEORGE DANDIN   Aha, crocodile! Licking your victim before you sink your teeth into him . . .

ANGELIQUE   For the last time . . .

GEORGE DANDIN   Enough. I'm implacable.

ANGELIQUE   Prove how open-minded you can be.

GEORGE DANDIN   No.

ANGELIQUE   Please!

GEORGE DANDIN   I will not.

ANGELIQUE   I implore you with all my soul.

GEORGE DANDIN   No! No! No! I want you seen in your true colors. I want you shamed in public.

ANGELIQUE   Well, if you're going to drive me to despair, I warn you that a woman in that state is capable of any deed. I'll do something you'll be sorry for.

GEORGE DANDIN   And what, exactly?

ANGELIQUE   I'll force myself to take the final decision. I'll kill myself with this knife.

GEORGE DANDIN   Ha, ha! Very good.

ANGELIQUE   Not so good as you think — for you. Everybody nearby knows of our differences and the grievances you hold against me. When I'm found dead, nobody will doubt that you killed me. And my parents won't let my death go unpunished. They'll hate you and insist on the severest penalty. That will be my retaliation. I won't be the first young person, far from it, who resorted to this type of vengeance. And I won't find it hard to die if I destroy somebody callous enough to have pushed me to the limit.

GEORGE DANDIN   I beg your pardon. People today don't kill themselves. Doing that went out of fashion long ago.

ANGELIQUE Remember what you're saying. It'll sound very cynical later. If you won't soften, if you don't open that door, I swear I'll make you see how far a woman can go when she's in despair.

GEORGE DANDIN Hot air, hot air. This is only to frighten me.

ANGELIQUE It's come to this, then: we both want it, and you'll see whether I was pretending. *(She flashes the knife.)* Aah! It's done! May heaven avenge my death according to my wishes, and may the man who's responsible meet with his punishment for treating me so harshly.

GEORGE DANDIN *(Aside)* She could never be malicious enough to kill herself in order to get me hanged. Or could she? Where's that candle? I'll take a quick look. *(He pulls his head in from the window.)*

ANGELIQUE *(To Claudine)* Psst! Quiet. We'll wait on either side of the doorway.

GEORGE DANDIN *(In the doorway, a stub of candle in his hand)* Could any woman be that spiteful? *(He steps out into the darkness. Angelique and Claudine slip inside and bolt the door.)* Nobody here. That's what I expected. She ran off. She saw she couldn't make any headway with me either by begging or threatening. All the better! That'll make her look even worse, and when her father and mother arrive they'll see her guilt that much more clearly. *(He tries to get back into the house.)* Oh, the door's shut. Ho, there, somebody, open up for me right away.

ANGELIQUE *(At the window, with Claudine)* What? Is that you? Where have you been, you degenerate? Is this any time to come home, almost at daybreak? Is this any way for a decent husband to behave?

CLAUDINE Nice goings-on — out carousing all night and leaves his poor young wife alone like this in the house.

GEORGE DANDIN What! You have the gall —

ANGELIQUE Go on, you debauched creature. I'm sick of your behavior, and I'm going to complain to my father and mother.

GEORGE DANDIN   You actually dare —

Re-enter Colin, holding a lantern, and followed by Monsieur and Madame de Sotenville in nightgowns.

ANGELIQUE   Thank heaven! Come here and pass judgment for me on this man, the most impossible husband ever. His brain is so addled with wine and jealousy he doesn't know any more what he's saying or doing. He sent for you himself to let you witness the most extravagant ravings. See, here he is, just come home after keeping me waiting all night. Look at his shirt tails! If you bother to listen to him he says he'll accuse me of having done horrible things, such as leaving him while he was asleep and wandering off out of doors, and other lies of the same kind.

GEORGE DANDIN   *(Aside)*   Wicked bitch!

CLAUDINE   Yes, he tried to pretend that he was in the house and we were outside. Seems there's no way to shake this stupid idea out of his head.

MONSIEUR DE SOTENVILLE   Indeed! What does this mean?

MADAME DE SOTENVILLE   The impudence of him! To bring us here for that!

GEORGE DANDIN   Never —

ANGELIQUE   Please, father, I can't bear having him for a husband. My patience has run out. He just finished insulting and cursing me.

MONSIEUR DE SOTENVILLE   By God, you're a vile man.

CLAUDINE   What a disgrace to see a poor young lady abused like that! It cries out to heaven for vengeance.

GEORGE DANDIN   Is it possible —?

MONSIEUR DE SOTENVILLE   Enough. You ought to die of shame.

GEORGE DANDIN   Let me say a couple of words —

ANGELIQUE   Listen to him. He'll tell you some colorful stories.

GEORGE DANDIN *(Aside)* I'm going frantic.

CLAUDINE He's soaked up so much wine I don't think you can go near him. We can smell it on his breath from up here.

GEORGE DANDIN Father-in-law — monsieur — I beseech you —

MONSIEUR DE SOTENVILLE Stand back! You reek of wine.

GEORGE DANDIN Madame, if I tell you —

MADAME DE SOTENVILLE Help! Don't come near me! Your breath is poisonous.

GEORGE DANDIN But monsieur, won't you let me —?

MONSIEUR DE SOTENVILLE Back, I said! You're disgusting.

GEORGE DANDIN Madame, if you give me the chance to —

MADAME DE SOTENVILLE Ech! You turn my stomach. Speak from over there, will you?

GEORGE DANDIN *(Retreating)* Very well. I'll speak from here. I swear I didn't budge from the house. She's the one who went out.

ANGÉLIQUE What did I tell you?

CLAUDINE It looks likely, doesn't it?

MONSIEUR DE SOTENVILLE *(To George Dandin)* It's revolting how you make fun of people. Daughter, come down here.

Angélique and Claudine disappear from the window.

GEORGE DANDIN I swear to God I was in the house and —

MADAME DE SOTENVILLE Silence! It's not true. You have no evidence.

GEORGE DANDIN May lightning strike me this instant if — !

MONSIEUR DE SOTENVILLE Stop giving us a headache, and prepare to ask your wife's forgiveness.

GEORGE DANDIN I'm to ask her forgiveness?

MONSIEUR DE SOTENVILLE Forgiveness, exactly. With no more haggling.

GEORGE DANDIN What —?

MONSIEUR DE SOTENVILLE Great God, if you keep resisting your duty I'll thump it into you by main force.

Angélique and Claudine come out of the house.

GEORGE DANDIN *(Aside)* Oh, George Dandin!

MONSIEUR DE SOTENVILLE Here, my girl. Your husband's going to beg your forgiveness.

ANGELIQUE I'm to forgive him, after what he said to me? No, father, I couldn't bring myself to do that. I must have a separation. Please! I can't live with the man any more.

CLAUDINE How can you refuse her?

MONSIEUR DE SOTENVILLE My child, separations can't be carried out without a great deal of scandal. You must show that you're wiser than he is and be patient once more.

ANGELIQUE How, after so much provocation? No, father, I can't go along with this.

MONSIEUR DE SOTENVILLE You must, my child. It's my command.

ANGELIQUE That word silences me. You have absolute power over my life.

CLAUDINE Such a sweet disposition!

ANGELIQUE It hurts to have to swallow insults like those, but even if I suffer for it, I'm incapable of disobeying you.

CLAUDINE Poor lamb!

MONSIEUR DE SOTENVILLE Stand here, my girl.

ANGELIQUE Whatever you make me do will count for nothing. Tomorrow, you'll see, it will start all over again.

MONSIEUR DE SOTENVILLE We'll take care of that. *(To George Dandin)* You! Down on your knees!

GEORGE DANDIN Not on my knees!

MONSIEUR DE SOTENVILLE On your knees! Now!

GEORGE DANDIN *(Kneeling, aside)* Oh God! Monsieur, what do I say?

MONSIEUR DE SOTENVILLE Madame, I beg you to forgive me . . .

GEORGE DANDIN "Madame, I beg you to forgive me . . ."

MONSIEUR DE SOTENVILLE For my ridiculous behavior. . .

GEORGE DANDIN "For my ridiculous behavior . . ." *(Aside)* . . . in marrying you.

MONSIEUR DE SOTENVILLE And I promise to improve in the future.

GEORGE DANDIN "And I promise to improve in the future."

MONSIEUR DE SOTENVILLE Make sure you do. This is the last impertinence we'll tolerate from you.

MADAME DE SOTENVILLE God on high! If you fail once again we'll make you learn the hard way how much respect you owe your wife and her forebears.

MONSIEUR DE SOTENVILLE It's growing light. Daybreak. Goodby. *(To George Dandin)* Go indoors and learn to live sensibly. *(To Madame de Sotenville)* Come, my love, home and to bed.

Exeunt everybody but George Dandin.

GEORGE DANDIN I give up. I see no remedy. Once you've married an evil wife like mine, the only way out is to throw yourself head-first into deep water.

THE END

THE MISER

(L'Avare)

Harpagon, in love with Mariane
Cléante, Harpagon's son, also in love with Mariane
Elise, Harpagon's daughter, in love with Valère
Valère, Anselme's son, in love with Elise
Mariane, Anselme's daughter, in love with Cléante
Anselme, father of Valère and Mariane
Maître Jacques, Harpagon's chef and coachman
Frosine, a matchmaker
La Flèche, Cléante's servant
Simon, a loan broker
Commissioner of police

Scene: A spacious downstairs room in Harpagon's house.

PART ONE

Elise and Valère.

VALERE Elise, my darling, you keep sighing. Are you sad because I'm happy? Do you regret our engagement?

ELISE I sigh because I'm afraid. I probably love you more than I should.

VALERE You're afraid? Of your feelings for me?

ELISE What will my father say? The family? Friends? Other people? And you — I'm unsure of you. A man often turns cool when he knows a woman loves him too warmly.

VALERE Don't judge me by others. Suspect me of anything but being lukewarm. I'll love you until the second I die.

ELISE All men say the same words. You prove yourself different by your actions.

VALERE Trust me, my dearest. Give me time. My actions will speak for themselves. Live for my hopes, not your fears.

ELISE I want to believe in you — so much! I think back to the day when you saved me from drowning. You snatched me out of the waves. You risked your life for mine. Since then, I have loved you for staying here with me, away from your family and your country. And you gave up your social rank for me. Yes, I know how much you've sacrificed. But how do others see you? As I do? No, they look on you as a servant.

VALERE Let them. Once I find my family again — and I intend to — everybody will be won over, your father included.

ELISE He's so suspicious.

VALERE   Avaricious. That slipped out. Forgive me for saying it,
my precious one, even if it's true. What's the answer, then? Shall I
leave? Shall I go off and search for my relatives so that I can prove
who I am?

ELISE   No, no! Stay. Give yourself time until father learns to
appreciate you as I do.

VALERE   You must have noticed how I've worked my way into his
good graces. I pretend to share his opinions and feelings. I'm
making surprising headway. I've discovered how to win a man's
confidence. You keep agreeing with him, nod and nod until your
neck aches — thoughtfully, of course. You praise his faults. You
applaud his mistakes. It's impossible to overdo the gush. Even a
killjoy turns pathetically grateful when you flatter him. Nothing's
too outrageous to cram down his gullet when you season it with
compliments. I admit that I cut the corners of sincerity. When you
need the help of others, you adjust yourself to them. That's how
you win them over. So don't blame the one who flatters; blame the
one who wants to *be* flattered.

ELISE   Shouldn't we seek help from my brother, in case he hears
about our secret from the housemaid?

VALERE   He and your father are so different in temperament that I
doubt whether I could deal with them both at the same time. But
remain friendly with him. You're fond of one another, aren't you?
By all means talk to him about us. Just don't let out more than you
have to. Perhaps he'll come over to our side. It's worth a try.
There — he's coming. Do what you can, my beloved.

He kisses her and goes out. Enter Cléante.

CLEANTE   Found you alone at last! My own, dearest sister! I have
a secret. The most important secret I ever gave away.

ELISE   A secret? What is it?

CLEANTE   A world of wonders wrapped up in one word — love.

ELISE   You're in love?

CLEANTE   I'm in love. Yes, I realize that I must submit to father's
wishes. He gave me life, didn't he? God appointed him master of

me and my desires. And I realize that fathers are not swayed by ridiculous impulses like love. They're too sensible. Not gullible, like us. They clearly see what's best for their blind offspring. And so we must respect father's intelligent judgment and not our own reckless, raw stupidity.

ELISE You don't have to lecture me.

CLEANTE I say this because I don't want you to say it. I don't want to hear it. I don't want to hear anything. I'm in love.

ELISE Engaged?

CLEANTE Not yet, but I've made up my mind. Please don't discourage me.

ELISE What am I, a father?

CLEANTE You're not in love. I'm afraid of your commonsense.

ELISE Let's not talk about my commonsense. Everybody runs short of that at least once in a lifetime. If I tell you about my own feelings you'll never call me sensible again.

CLEANTE You're in trouble too?

ELISE We'll discuss your affair first. Who is she?

CLEANTE Her name is Mariane. She's new to the neighborhood. A superb, inspiring girl! She waits on her invalid mother so sensitively it would touch you to the soul. The charm she has! And her movements, her gestures! She's gentle and bewitching, invitingly, lovably modest and — oh, my darling sister, if you could only meet her. . .

ELISE You love her. That's enough to convince me.

CLEANTE They're poor and they live frugally. What a joy it would be to raise the fortunes of the woman I love, and to help her and her mother by providing some of the small necessities of life. I mean, discreetly. And now imagine how bad I feel. Because father's a miser, I don't have what I need to prove how much I love this lovely girl.

ELISE   I understand your bitterness.

CLEANTE   It's beyond understanding. That tightwad! His fist
closes on us like a vise. We languish in these sterile surroundings.
What good will it do us to inherit his money when we're too
decrepit to enjoy it? I scratch around for loans on every side,
simply to stay alive. Each day I have to ask tradespeople for credit
so I can dress decently. All because of him. If he doesn't give me
permission to marry my angel, we'll elope and manage as best we
can with whatever providence sends us. I'm doing my utmost to
borrow money that'll enable us to leave and break free of his
unbearable meanness. And if he opposes you, too, we'll take you
with us.

ELISE   It's terrible. He gives us more and more reasons to wish
poor mother were still alive.

Harpagon is heard offstage.

CLEANTE   That's his voice. Let's step out of sight and finish
talking.

As Elise and Cléante leave, Harpagon arrives with La Flèche.

HARPAGON   Don't talk back to me! Out of my house, you limping
wreck, you prowling scrounger, you apology for a thief!

LA FLECHE   *(Aside)* He's the devil. *(Looking toward heaven)*
Forgive me for saying so.

HARPAGON   Are you whispering to yourself?

LA FLECHE   Why do you keep picking on me?

HARPAGON   He answers me back again! Out, out!

LA FLECHE   Your son is my master, and he ordered me to wait
here.

HARPAGON   Wait in the street, not in my home, where you stick out
of the floor like a crooked post with eyeballs, watching everything
that goes on and hoping to make something out of it. I won't have
you in front of me all the time, or behind me. You scuttle into every
corner, like a crippled spider, for things to rob me of.

LA FLECHE   I could never rob you. You're not robbable. You lock up all your stuff and guard it day and night.

HARPAGON   Snoopers, felons, in my own home!   You're just the one, with your slippery, twisted tongue to start a rumor that I have money hidden.

LA FLECHE   You have money hidden?

HARPAGON   Who said that?

LA FLECHE   Said what?

HARPAGON   That I have money hidden.

LA FLECHE   Have you?

HARPAGON   I didn't say I *have*.

LA FLECHE   What's it to me?   I never see any of your money.

HARPAGON   Now you want to argue, hey?   How's this for an argument? *(Raises his fist.)*

LA FLECHE   I'm going.

HARPAGON   Stop!   What are you taking?

LA FLECHE   Am I taking something?

HARPAGON   Don't move. Hold out your hands.

LA FLECHE   Here.

HARPAGON   And the others!

LA FLECHE   My other hands?

HARPAGON   What did you hide in your breeches?

LA FLECHE   See for yourself.

HARPAGON   *(Seeing for himself)*   These baggy garments were
made for concealing stolen property. The tailor should have been
sewn up in them and dropped in the river.

LA FLECHE   *(Aside)*   This is one man I really would love to rob.

HARPAGON   What was that about robbing?

LA FLECHE   I said, you really poke around to see if you were
robbed.

HARPAGON   I haven't started yet.   *(He burrows in La Flèche's
pockets.)*

LA FLECHE   *(Muttering)*   A pox on all skinflints!

HARPAGON   What was that about skinflints?

LA FLECHE   A pox on them all.

HARPAGON   What are you referring to?

LA FLECHE   Misers.

HARPAGON   What misers?

LA FLECHE   You don't think I'm talking about you?

HARPAGON   I know what I think.   Tell me exactly what you meant.

LA FLECHE   I never name names.

HARPAGON   I'll cut off your good leg, you stinking criminal.

LA FLECHE   Whoever smells dung, let him blow his own nose.
Look, here's a pocket you missed.

HARPAGON   Last chance: give it up!

LA FLECHE   Give what up?

HARPAGON   What you took from me, cockroach.

LA FLECHE   I didn't take a thing.

HARPAGON You did.

LA FLECHE I didn't

HARPAGON You did!

LA FLECHE I didn't!

HARPAGON You — go to hell, you lame dog!

LA FLECHE Thanks for the blessing. *(Exit.)*

HARPAGON Don't go through the garden! *(Alone)* It's a burden having a great sum of money on your hands. The ideal strategy is to invest your nest-egg, keep it nicely positioned for high, steady dividends, while you hold onto only the amount you need for daily transactions. But how can you store it? The unsafest place for money is a safe. It actually attracts your average burglar. It's the first thing he goes for. So I asked myself: Where could I stow away those fifty thousand crowns I took in yesterday? One hundred gold coins, legal tender, very tender. Very plump. In a cash box? Locked up? And buried? Aha! In the garden! It seemed logical at the time. But last night — oh, what a night! — I tossed, I fretted, I wept. Suppose some dog comes sniffing by and uproots the whole box? Or the gardeners start planting bulbs? Or somebody notices that the earth is soft, even though I stamped it down so that the spot is invisible? Invisible! Will I ever find it again? Fifty thousand little crowns, alone, lost out there, growing cold... *(Re-enter Elise and Cléante.)* What did I say? Did I give the whole thing away? I mustn't get excited. What was that, my boy?

CLEANTE I didn't speak, father.

HARPAGON Have you two been there long?

ELISE We just came in.

HARPAGON You heard?

CLEANTE Heard what?

HARPAGON You did, you did!

ELISE   Did we?

HARPAGON   I was thinking aloud. These days it's not easy to come by hard cash, and I thought, Happy is the man who has fifty thousand crowns.

CLEANTE   We were chatting over there.

HARPAGON   Don't misinterpret my innocent words. I'm not the one who has fifty thousand crowns.

CLEANTE   We never pry into your business.

HARPAGON   Who doesn't wish to have fifty thousand crowns?

ELISE   I don't know.

HARPAGON   Wouldn't you like fifty thousand crowns?

CLEANTE   I don't believe —

HARPAGON   You could make good use of fifty thousand crowns, couldn't you? So could I. And all of us. What a dream — fifty thousand crowns!

ELISE   We wanted to ask you —

HARPAGON   With fifty thousand crowns I'd never need to complain.

CLEANTE   Father, you have no reason to complain now. Everyone knows you're well off.

HARPAGON   Me? Well off? People who say things like that are perjuring themselves. They ought to be locked up. In jail, not in a cash box. They're the dregs of society, they are, the liars who spread these pernicious stories.

ELISE   Don't lose your temper.

HARPAGON   This is frightening. My own children shouting to the world that I'm wealthy — my children, my enemies.

CLEANTE   Is it being your enemy to mention that you're well off?

HARPAGON Yes. Someone will take me for a gold mine. Talk like that will get my throat cut one of these days. So will these heavy expenses you let yourself in for.

CLEANTE Which heavy expenses?

HARPAGON For example, this outfit of yours. I told your sister off yesterday, but this is worse, more sumptuous. Take you from hat to shoes, you're wearing enough there to pay for a life annuity. My boy, I've said this twenty times: to go dressed up as you are now, aping tomorrow's fashions, you must be robbing me.

CLEANTE How could I possibly rob you?

HARPAGON Where else do you get the funds to parade through the town in such luxury?

CLEANTE I gamble. I've been lucky. All my winnings go into clothes.

HARPAGON If you're lucky at gambling, make the most of it. Let the proceeds earn a respectable interest so that one day when you need, you have. What's the point of those silks, those flimsy items you're swaddled in from sternum to cranium? And how much did you pay for that tangle of bramble that represents itself as a haircut? Why this insensate urge to splurge? I'll wager you've spent over two hundred crowns on this frippery. At a meager eight-and-a-quarter per cent, those two hundred would bring you each year exactly seventeen point nine eight three six five crowns in dividends.

CLEANTE It sounds right.

HARPAGON We'll let that go and come to another matter. Now what's all this winking and nodding? Are you two exchanging secrets? What are those signals for?

ELISE We were wondering who should speak first. We both have something to say to you.

HARPAGON And I have something to say to both of you. About marriage.

ELISE Marriage!

HARPAGON   Marriage. Is it the word that shocks you, my girl, or the thing?

CLEANTE   We hope our desires won't clash with yours.

HARPAGON   Why should they? Listen patiently. Calm yourselves. I'm perfectly aware of what you both need. You won't regret my plans. To begin at the beginning. Have you observed a young person who lives not far from here named Mariane?

CLEANTE   Yes, father.

HARPAGON   And you?

ELISE   I've heard of her.

HARPAGON   My son, what do you think of this girl?

CLEANTE   A very pleasing young woman.

HARPAGON   Her looks?

CLEANTE   Fresh and lively.

HARPAGON   Her air, her manner?

CLEANTE   Well above average. *Very* attractive.

HARPAGON   And she'd make a desirable match?

CLEANTE   Most desirable.

HARPAGON   She could become an efficient housekeeper?

CLEANTE   No question.

HARPAGON   And a man could find ah, satisfaction with her?

CLEANTE   Definitely.

HARPAGON   There's one complication. She has no money.

CLEANTE   Money doesn't count for much, father, when you're marrying a lovable person.

HARPAGON I beg your pardon, I beg your pardon. Still, if you don't find all the resources you hoped for, possibly you can make it up some other way.

CLEANTE That goes without saying.

HARPAGON So . . . I'm very glad you share my feelings, because her upright character and her gentleness have captivated me, and provided I can find something of a dowry there, I've made up my mind to marry her.

CLEANTE Oh!

HARPAGON What is it?

CLEANTE You say you've made up your mind . . .?

HARPAGON To marry Mariane.

CLEANTE What, you? You? You!!

HARPAGON Yes. I, I, I. What's wrong?

CLEANTE All of a sudden I feel dizzy. I'd better get some air.

HARPAGON You're not sick? Go and pour yourself a large glass of fresh water. *(Exit Cléante.)* So much for your delicate fops. They have no more stamina than chickens. And that, my daughter, is what I've decided on for myself. For your brother I've settled on a widow I learned about last night. She's not well — fading fast, in fact — but she has most of her teeth and hair left, more than half, and a substantial endowment from her late husband. Better than gambling, hey? As for you, I'm giving you to Anselme.

ELISE Not Count Anselme!

HARPAGON That's right: a steady, cautious, sensible nobleman, not overripe in years — barely fifty — and not an impoverished boy — a man. With an income that's widely admired.

ELISE *(Curtseying)* Please, father, I don't want to marry.

HARPAGON *(Curtseying back)* Please, daughter, I want you to marry.

ELISE   I'm sorry, father.

HARPAGON   I'm determined, daughter.

ELISE   I have nothing against Count Anselme —

HARPAGON   I have nothing but your best interests at heart —

ELISE   No, I will not marry him.

HARPAGON   Yes, you will marry him. This evening.

ELISE   This evening?

HARPAGON   This very evening.

ELISE   You'll never inflict him on me, father.

HARPAGON   I will, daughter. Before the daylight dims.

ELISE   I'll kill myself sooner than take such a husband.

HARPAGON   I will not permit you to kill yourself. You shall wed him. The impudence! Did anybody ever hear a daughter speak to her father like this?

ELISE   Did anybody ever see a father marry off his daughter like this?

HARPAGON   No reasonable person could object to this match.

ELISE   I say any reasonable person would object to it.

HARPAGON   Here comes Valère. Will you let him give us his impartial judgment?

ELISE   I'll accept that.

HARPAGON   You'll abide by his decision?

ELISE   Yes. Whatever he says.

Enter Valère.

HARPAGON   It's an agreement! Here, my friend, we've chosen you to say which of us is right, my daughter or I.

VALERE   You.

HARPAGON   You don't know why we differ.

VALERE   No, but you couldn't be wrong.

HARPAGON   I'm giving my daughter a husband.

VALERE   A husband!

HARPAGON   This evening.

VALERE   That soon!

HARPAGON   He's rich, generous, and well born. But this stupid, spoiled girl doesn't want him. What do you say to that?

VALERE   What do I say?

HARPAGON   Yes. Speak up.

VALERE   I say that ah, you can't help being right.

ELISE   Oh!

VALERE   On the other hand, she's not altogether wrong, because —

HARPAGON   We can't both be right, can we?

VALERE   Not exactly, but —

HARPAGON   I've fixed her up with Count Anselme. He's a formidable match. Fifty sprightly years of age, and a widower like me.

VALERE   Fifty years old!

HARPAGON   Young. Better yet, there's no child from his other marriage. She'll inherit everything.

VALERE   Capital!   But perhaps she needs a few days, or weeks, or months, to think this over —

HARPAGON   No thinking over. This is an opportunity, and urgent. He's prepared to take her with no dowry.

VALERE   No dowry. Then I'm silent. *(To Elise)*   That's the conclusive point. *(To Harpagon)*   Still, your daughter might claim that marriage is a serious commitment. It determines whether she'll be happy or unhappy for the rest of her life.

HARPAGON   But no dowry!

VALERE   That answers all objections. No dowry. Yet some people might say that her preferences ought to be taken into account, and that, given the gulf between her age and his, and a possible incompatibility — the differences in their personality —

HARPAGON   No dowry.

VALERE   No dowry. Who can challenge no dowry? All the same, some fathers care more for the welfare of their daughters than for the money they have to part with. Such loving parents will seek a marriage in which the two young people love each other.

HARPAGON   No —

VALERE   — Dowry. That chokes off all qualifying clauses, doesn't it?

HARPAGON   *(Aside)*   Did I hear a dog bark in the garden? Someone's after my cash box. *(Aloud)*   Wait. I'll be right back. *(Exit.)*

ELISE   How could you pander to him like that?

VALERE   If I oppose him I'll damage our plans. Some temperaments, like his, can't bear opposition. And the truth angers them. You must lead them by roundabout routes. Pretend to give in and you'll find —

ELISE   But this marriage!

VALERE   We'll break it off.   Somehow.

ELISE By this evening?

VALERE Ask for a delay. Say you're ill.

ELISE He'll call in a doctor.

VALERE What does a doctor know? Dream up any symptoms you want; he always has a disease to match them — and an expensive treatment.

Re-enter Harpagon.

HARPAGON *(Aside)* False alarm, thank God.

VALERE If we can't stop the marriage, we'll run away, put ourselves out of his reach. Oh, my dear, dear — *(He notices Harpagon.)* My dear, dear young lady, a daughter always obeys her father. And when she also faces the overpowering appeal of *no dowry,* she accepts what she's given, with thanks.

HARPAGON Good. Very well put, that.

VALERE Forgive me, monsieur, if I got carried away and spoke to her so boldly.

HARPAGON No, I approve. I want you to exercise full power over her. Elise, I confer on him the authority vested by heaven in me. Valère, don't let her out of your sight.

VALERE I'll stay close to her and give her more instructions.

HARPAGON I'm obliged to you.

VALERE It's wise to keep a tight hold on her. I think I know how to win her confidence.

HARPAGON Do that. I have an appointment. I'll be back shortly.

VALERE Yes, money is more precious than anything else. Your father knows what makes the world go around. *No dowry* is the be-all and end-all. It takes the place of good looks, youth, honor, wisdom, and integrity. *(He escorts Elise out.)*

HARPAGON   An oracle!   He has a golden tongue.   What a loyal servant!   *(Exit.)*

[THIS IS THE END OF ACT ONE.]

Enter Cléante and La Flèche.

CLEANTE   So there you are, slug.   Where did you crawl off to? Didn't I order you to wait for me?

LA FLECHE   I stood here for ages.   Then your father came in, abused me, searched me, very nearly attacked me, and shoved me outside.

CLEANTE   How's our business coming along?   We must move fast.   I just found out that he's my rival for Mariane.

LA FLECHE   Your father?   Don't tell me he's in love.   Is he trying to disguise himself as a human being?

CLEANTE   I'm already in enough difficulties.   Any luck with our loan?

LA FLECHE   When you borrow money, luck doesn't come into it.

CLEANTE   The deal won't go through?

LA FLECHE   I didn't say that.   This man Simon, the broker they assigned to us, says he'll go to any length to get what you want — he likes your face.

CLEANTE   Will I have the full twelve thousand?

LA FLECHE   Certainly.   With a clause or two attached.

CLEANTE   Did you speak to the lender?

LA FLECHE   It doesn't work like that.   I have no idea who the lender is, couldn't even pick up a hint of his name.   But he wants to meet you somewhere today, not here, on neutral ground.   He'll ask about your assets and family background.   I wouldn't be surprised if your father's name alone smoothed the way for us.

CLEANTE And even more, my mother's legacy. Nobody can take that away from me.

LA FLECHE Here are the provisions in a contract he dictated to our broker. You'll have to sign this:

"Provided that the lender be privy to all his security, and that the borrower be of age and from a family whose assets are ample, sound, assured, clear, and free from all claims, a valid and detailed bond shall be drawn up before a lawyer, a man of the highest character, chosen for this purpose by the lender."

CLEANTE Nothing to quarrel with so far.

LA FLECHE "The lender, in order not to weigh down his conscience, will supply his money at a rate not exceeding five-and-one-half per cent."

CLEANTE What's that again? Only five-and-a-half? There's honesty for you! No complaints on that score.

LA FLECHE And here's a sub-clause:

"But as the said lender does not have the agreed-upon sum readily available and is compelled, for the sake of the borrower, to secure it elsewhere, it is only fair that said borrower defray this additional interest, which runs at twenty per cent."

CLEANTE Another twenty! Who is this extortioner? That adds up to more than twenty-five per cent.

LA FLECHE You'd better sleep on it.

CLEANTE How can I? I need the money today. I'll have to say yes.

LA FLECHE That's what I told them.

CLEANTE Oh God! Anything else?

LA FLECHE One more clause:

"Of the twelve thousand requested, the lender is able to supply only nine thousand in cash. The borrower must accept the balance of three thousand in antiques, home furnishings, and valuables, priced with due moderation."

CLEANTE   What's this about?

LA FLECHE   "The inventory includes one bed, forty-eight inches in length —"

CLEANTE   Forty-eight inches!   Is that a crib? Or a bed for a midget?

LA FLECHE   "— With Hungarian lace point trappings, finely appliqué'd. Also one bedspread lined with shot taffeta. Next: one curtained canopy having long and short tassels —"

CLEANTE   I don't believe this.

LA FLECHE   Wait. "Next: one set of tapestries depicting a scene of pastoral love, with cherubs, deer, squirrels, birds of colorful plumage, and many acres of spacious landscape. Next: one large walnut table with twelve shaped legs, pull-outs at both ends, and matching stools —"

CLEANTE   Where in God's name can I store all this rubbish?

LA FLECHE   We haven't finished. "Next: three oversized muskets inlaid with mother-of-pearl. Next: one brick furnace with two retort flasks, most serviceable for those whose hobby is distilling."

CLEANTE   I'm losing my mind.

LA FLECHE   *(Scanning the sheet)*   What else? "One Bolognese lute with nearly all its strings. One Find-the-Lady gaming table, one children's toy called Goosey-Goosey —"

CLEANTE   Goosey-Goosey!

LA FLECHE   "Next: one lizard skin, forty-two inches in length and stuffed with straw, a delightful curio for hanging from a ceiling. The total value of these precious acquisitions exceeds forty-five hundred crowns, but by the lender's discretion is reduced to the said three thousand."

CLEANTE Him and his discretion! The pirate! The piranha! He's not satisfied with his insane percentage. For three thousand crowns he forces me to clean out his attic. I won't get a hundred for the lot. And yet I must say yes. The murderer has me with a knife at my throat.

LA FLECHE No offense, monsieur, but as the poet says, when you ask for money in advance, you're on the road to ruin: You buy dear, you sell cheap, and eat your own corn while it's still green.

CLEANTE This is what I'm stuck with because of a stingy father. No wonder sons like me sometimes wish fathers like him dead.

LA FLECHE His greed and money-grubbing would enrage the calmest man. I'm no crook, God knows, and I'm not eager to risk a rope around the neck the way a lot of my shady acquaintances in the profession do. But in this case I could easily be tempted; and if I did rob him I'd be doing what's only right and fair.

CLEANTE Let me look over that list again.

While they are talking, Harpagon enters with Simon.

SIMON Yes, he's a young fellow and he's badly in need of ready money. He'll sign the contract.

HARPAGON Listen, Simon, don't you think I face some risk here? Do you know his name, family, and resources?

SIMON I can't give you the particulars. Somebody introduced us. But his man assures me you'll find everything satisfactory. He comes from a wealthy family. His mother's already dead, and he'll certify, if you wish, that within eight months he'll also bury his father.

HARPAGON That's a good start. The spirit of charity, my dear Simon, obliges us, whenever we can, to show others a helping hand and an open heart.

SIMON God knows, that's true.

LA FLECHE What's going on? There's our broker talking to your father.

CLEANTE   You told him who I am!

LA FLECHE   No, I swear it.

SIMON   *(To La Flèche)*   This is an awkward surprise. Who told
you the appointment was here?   *(To Harpagon)*   I have no idea
who gave them your address, monsieur, but there's no harm done.
They're here, they're eager, they're discreet.   Now for the contract.

HARPAGON   What!

SIMON   This gentleman is the borrower. The twelve thousand . . .
the clauses.

HARPAGON   I don't believe this. *(To Cléante)*   So you're the idiot!

CLEANTE   And you're the bloodsucker!

They each raise a fist. Simon and La Flèche leave rapidly.

HARPAGON   You're trying to ruin yourself with outrageous loans.

CLEANTE   You're trying to bloat yourself on immoral interest.

HARPAGON   How can you stand here and face me?

CLEANTE   How can you go out and face the world?

HARPAGON   Aren't you ashamed of sinking into this debauchery,
these horrifying expenses, and scattering the resources scraped
together by the sweat of your parents?

CLEANTE   Don't you blush at having dishonored your name by
giving in to this mania for piling gold on gold?

HARPAGON   Out of my sight!

CLEANTE   Who's worse, the man who buys money because he
must have it or the man who fleeces others for money he doesn't
need?

HARPAGON   Out, I said!   *(Exit Cléante.)*   An interesting
coincidence.   It'll teach me to keep an even closer watch on him.

Enter Frosine.

FROSINE   Good morning, monsieur!

HARPAGON   Did you come in through the garden?

FROSINE   I always come in through the garden.

HARPAGON   Who gave you permission to come in through the garden?

He rushes out into the garden.

La Flèche comes out of hiding.

LA FLECHE   This is hilarious. The old pinchpenny has a ton of junk stashed away somewhere. I didn't recognize any of the things in his inventory.

FROSINE   La Flèche, sweetie!   How are things?

LA FLECHE   Frosine!   *(They kiss.)*   What are you doing here?

FROSINE   What I do everywhere, racing back and forth between clients, doing good to everybody, loving the wide world and helping the world find love. Making the most of my rare gifts. People in my profession, you know, we have to work to the limit to survive, and the only capital heaven supplies us with is a genius for planning.

LA FLECHE   Are you doing something for the old money-monger?

FROSINE   Yes, I've set up an arrangement, for the usual commission.

LA FLECHE   Commission? From him? You're joking.

FROSINE   There are some services that pay off.

LA FLECHE   You don't know Harpagon. No service strains his gratitude enough to make him unclench his fingers. Praise, yes; respect, kind wishes, and chummy smiles — as much of them as you want. But money? Not a hope. Why, he detests the word *give*. He never gives you a good morning; he only lends it.

FROSINE I've learned the art of milking men. I know how to unlock their good will, tickle their hearts, sneak into their sensitive zones.

LA FLECHE A waste of time here. He's a stone. You could shatter him sooner than move him. Just seeing one person ask another for cash sends him into convulsions. If you or I — never mind, here he is. I'm off. *(Exit.)*

Enter Harpagon.

HARPAGON *(Aside)* Nothing was touched. *(Aloud)* Yes, what is it, Frosine?

FROSINE My, don't you look fit! The picture of health.

HARPAGON Who, me?

FROSINE Frisky and bouncy, fresh complexion . . .

HARPAGON Seriously?

FROSINE You never looked this young in your life. I've seen lads of twenty-five who seem older than you.

HARPAGON You know, Frosine, I'm past sixty.

FROSINE Sixty? For you that's the age of opening up, like an oak tree.

HARPAGON Perhaps. But I wouldn't mind shedding twenty years.

FROSINE You're joking. You don't need that. You have what it takes to live to a hundred.

HARPAGON How can you tell?

FROSINE Look, there it is, right between your eyes, the mark of an abnormally long life. I said one hundred, but I told a fib. Now I can see you'll top one-twenty.

HARPAGON Is that possible?

FROSINE   They'll have to hit you over the head. You'll bury your children and your children's children.

HARPAGON   All the better. How's our business coming along?

FROSINE   Need you ask? I have this astounding knack for matching people. You won't find two creatures in creation that I couldn't couple. If I had a notion to do it, I could marry a chimp to a chinchilla. Not that there were any difficulties in this case. I'm friendly with the two women. I told the mother you took a liking to Mariane the first time you caught a glimpse of her at her window.

HARPAGON   And she answered . . .?

FROSINE   Couldn't be happier. *Loved* the proposal. And when I said you wanted me to invite Mariane here this afternoon for your daughter's wedding, the mother almost leaped out of her sick bed with joy.

HARPAGON   I'm compelled to give a supper for the bridegroom, Count Anselme, unfortunately, so why not have Mariane at the reception to meet my children and kill several birds with one stone?

FROSINE   Very thoughtful of you. She told me she's dying to come.

HARPAGON   You can collect her in my carriage. No sense in renting one. Now, did you say anything to the mother about giving the girl a lump sum? Did you make it clear that she has to stretch for an opportunity like this, make a tremendous effort, even bleed a little? Nobody marries a girl unless she brings in something.

FROSINE   Something? Twelve thousand a year.

HARPAGON   Twelve thousand! That much I didn't expect.

FROSINE   You see, she's a most unusual girl. *First,* she grew up on a scanty diet. She's used to living on salad, milk, cabbage, and bread. Result? She won't expect pheasant, steak, caviar, and exotic vegetables like asparagus and artichokes. Those delicacies, which married women dote on, can set you back three thousand crowns a year. *Second,* she cares only for simple clothes. She doesn't go in for showy ball gowns or high-priced jewels or high-stepping shoes. And there you save more than another four thousand a year. Three plus four! Seven thousand. *Third,* card games appall her, and today you find hardly any wives who don't play. One of them I heard of dropped twenty thousand last night. So add five thousand for gambling to the other seven for clothes, jewelry, and food, and there you have your twelve thousand, free and clear.

HARPAGON   The arithmetic is ingenious, but there's no substance in it.

FROSINE   Excuse me. No substance when she brings you a frugal appetite for a dowry, a simple taste in clothes for an inheritance, and a horror of gambling for a bonus?

HARPAGON   It's facetious to work me up a marriage invoice out of money she won't spend. I wouldn't give a receipt for goods not delivered. I want something I can put my hands on.

FROSINE   You'll have your hands *full.* The two of them told me about some country or other where they own property, resources, which you'll take over.

HARPAGON   That's to be seen. There's another thing that bothers me. The girl's young, and young women as a rule seek the company of young men. I'm afraid a man of my age won't suit her taste, and this could lead to complications of a . . . domestic and nocturnal character.

FROSINE   I told you she was unusual. Here's one more benefit I didn't mention. She hates young men. She loves old men.

HARPAGON   Actually loves them?

FROSINE   I wish you'd heard her on that subject. She admitted that the very sight of a young fellow grates on her. But a mature man, a full beard, and a bald head — these are what arouse her. The older a man is, the more he charms her. So I advise you not to make yourself out to be younger. Sixty is the bottom line. Several months ago she broke off an engagement when her fiancé confessed he was only fifty-six and didn't wear glasses. I told you she was unusual.

HARPAGON   Not too unusual, I hope?

FROSINE She can't help it. She would not come down to fifty-six.
And she enjoys looking at a man's nose when it has a pair of
spectacles perched on it.

HARPAGON *(Putting on his glasses)* That's what I call wisdom.
If I'd been a woman I wouldn't have liked young men.

FROSINE I believe it. A fine gaggle they are, the primping
peacocks. They expect us to gasp over their tails.

HARPAGON I can't fathom out why women waste time with them.

FROSINE Can you imagine loving one of those milksops? Are
they men, those pretty darlings?

HARPAGON With their simpering voices and cheap, easy
compliments, and wild hairstyles and laughable breeches and
newfangled boots and stitching on their silk shirts . . .

FROSINE They call that being well put-together — against someone
sturdy like you! Here's a man. Here's something mellow to make
a pair of eyes shine. Here's how to inspire a helpless, boundless
love!

HARPAGON You think I'm all right?

FROSINE Do I! You're made to be adored, to be painted. So
young!

HARPAGON Not too young!

FROSINE No, no! Let me see you walk. *(He walks self-
consciously.)* That's what I call a body. Lithe, upright, athletic as
it should be. Without one flaw.

HARPAGON No serious ailments, thank God, only a touch of
phlegm that catches at me now and then.

FROSINE Your phlegm suits you, and you cough magnificently.

HARPAGON One little question: Has Mariane seen me yet? Did she
notice me as I went past her house?

FROSINE We've talked endlessly about you. I gave her a full description, head to heels. She made me repeat it three times.

HARPAGON You did well, and I thank you.

FROSINE Now, monsieur, there's a teeny favor I want to ask. I have a lawsuit I may lose. All I need is a small sum, and you could turn the tide for me if — *(He frowns.)* She'll be so excited to see you. *(He smiles.)* Your poise, your posture. But most of all she'll admire your plain, correct dress. That will drive her crazy. A formal, mature lover, a treat.

HARPAGON You exaggerate. Slightly.

FROSINE But the fact is, monsieur, to me this lawsuit means life or death. If I lose, I'm ruined. *(He frowns.)* I wish you'd seen her when I explained the advantages of having a spouse like you. In raptures! *(He smiles.)* As I listed your qualities, she could hardly wait for the wedding night.

HARPAGON You've done me an unequaled service, Frosine. I'm forever in your debt.

FROSINE How about a small kindness in return, monsieur? To discharge the debt? *(He frowns.)* It'll put me back on my feet, and I'll be able to do even more for you.

HARPAGON I must go.

FROSINE On my oath, you'll never rescue any person from worse circumstances.

HARPAGON Did I hear rain out there? I'd better look, in case someone's taking shelter in my garden under my trees.

FROSINE I wouldn't dream of troubling you, except that this is an agonizing necessity.

HARPAGON That rain will collect in all the low-lying spots: puddles and pools and ponds ...

FROSINE Please don't turn me down! *(On her knees)* One act of mercy!

HARPAGON   Ponds, lakes, floods, torrents, soil erosion . . .
(Exit.)

FROSINE   May you rot, you son of Satan!   May your income dry
up!   May your savings hemorrhage and your loans fester!   How can
I squeeze my commission out of this weasel?   Let me think, think,
think up something diabolical . . . *(Exit.)*

[THIS IS THE END OF ACT TWO.]

*Lighting change.   Harpagon leads Cléante, Elise, Valère, La Flèche,
and Jacques on stage in a procession.*

HARPAGON   Orders for the day!   Line up here.   I'm about to assign
your duties.   *(To La Flèche)*   Step forward, you!   Since you're
still here, we'll keep you hopping.   You will clean everything, every
last thing.   Don't polish the furniture too hard and wear it down.
During the reception you will take command of all glassware.   If one
piece is missing or broken I'll hold you responsible and dock your
pay.

JACQUES   A sensible precaution.

HARPAGON   After washing the glasses, you will serve drinks, but
only to people who ask you several times.   Don't act like those
improvident lackeys who come around tempting the guests, sloshing
them into intoxication with repeated refills they didn't realize they
wanted.   And stir in plenty of refreshing water.

JACQUES   Ah, yes.   Sound advice.   Water eases constipation.

LA FLECHE   Do I take off my old overalls?

HARPAGON   Not until you see the company arriving.   Then you
won't soil your uniform beforehand.   And you'd better not soil it
after.

LA FLECHE   I've been telling you since last winter that I have a
great oil stain on the front of my jacket.   And I've worn holes in the
seat of my pants.   You can see right through to the, excuse my
slang, skin.   There's a horrible draft that flows all around —

HARPAGON Calm down. Stand with your back to the wall. Show the company your front. And hide the oil stain like so. *(He holds his hat in front of his stomach.)* Keep the plate in front of it while you're serving. But don't drop the plate! *(La Flèche is about to speak. Harpagon waves him out.)* As for you, daughter, you'll keep an eye on the leftovers and see that nothing edible is thrown away. That's critical training for a wife-to-be. Meanwhile, get yourself dressed to greet my fiancée. Try to look more attractive than you are. Understood?

ELISE Yes, father. *(Exit.)*

HARPAGON And you, my son the fop, I was generous enough to forgive you your recent trespasses, so don't make any more of those sour faces.

CLEANTE I, father? Sour faces?

HARPAGON Everyone knows how children react when their fathers marry again. They resent having a stepmother. If you want me to overlook your escapades, receive the young lady with a friendly expression. Like this.

CLEANTE I'd be lying if I said I'm pleased to have her as my stepmother. But I promise to obey you to the letter and pretend to welcome her warmly.

HARPAGON Make sure you pretend with genuine conviction. *(Exit Cléante.)* Valère, I want you to watch everyone and everything. Anticipate trouble. Don't let it happen.

VALERE Rest assured.

HARPAGON Now then, Jacques, I saved you till last.

JACQUES Do you wish to speak to your coachman, monsieur, or your chef?

HARPAGON Both of you.

JACQUES Which one first, monsieur?

HARPAGON The chef.

JACQUES One moment, please. *(Removes his coachman's overcoat. He is now dressed as a chef.)* Your chef is listening, monsieur.

HARPAGON Will you give us plenty to eat today?

JACQUES Yes, if you give me plenty of money.

HARPAGON Money, money all the time, money! They talk of nothing but money, money, money. It's the only word they have on their boring tongues: money. The same old refrain: money. The sword they keep under their pillows: money.

VALERE I never heard a more unpromising promise — to supply plenty of food for plenty of money. Any fool could manage that. Have you no experience, no imagination? Why can't you make a great meal with very little money?

JACQUES A great meal with very little money?

VALERE Precisely.

JACQUES Master Manager, you'll do us all a favor if you let us in on your secret recipes and take over from me as chef. You love to interfere in other people's work. What do you know about the cost of raw provisions?

HARPAGON That's enough of that. What will we need?

JACQUES Speak to Master Manager. He'll make you a great meal, monsieur, with very little money.

HARPAGON That'll do, I said. I'm waiting for an answer.

JACQUES How many will you be at table?

HARPAGON Eight or ten. In other words, food for eight will feed ten.

VALERE That goes without saying.

JACQUES   Well, then, we'll want soup, appetizers, fish, and a meat entrée, all the usual —

HARPAGON   Stop!   He thinks he's feeding a starving tribe. . .

JACQUES   Game, goose, a side of beef, mutton —

HARPAGON   *(Clapping a hand over his mouth)*   Glutton!   You're eating up my resources.

JACQUES   A reasonable choice of vegetables with sauces, a variety of hot and cold desserts —

HARPAGON   More yet!

VALERE   Do you want to make our guests sick?   Did we invite them here to eat or to burst?   Are you going to cram them to death? Ask the doctors if there's anything more dangerous than overeating.

HARPAGON   Ab-so-lutely.

VALERE   Ab-so-lutely.   It's time you found out, you and other hogs like you, that a table piled high with food is a lethal weapon.   To prove you really care about your guests, you give them a light, easily digestible snack.   In the words of the philosopher, "We must eat to live, not live to eat."

HARPAGON   I must hug you for that wise saying.   It's pithy, it's pregnant.   "We must live to eat, and not —"   Not what?   Say it again.

VALERE   Ab-so-lutely.   "We must eat to live, not live to eat."

HARPAGON   Jacques, did you hear?   Did you take it in?   What great man said that?

VALERE   His name escapes me for the moment.

HARPAGON   Write down those words.   I want them engraved in gold lettering over the fireplace in my dining room.

VALERE   Gold?

HARPAGON   Or copper.   Valère, could you take over the cooking?

VALERE Ab-so-lutely. Nothing easier.

HARPAGON Give us a dish that's filling, beans in lard and pie with a thick layer of soft dough and a lot of chestnut stuffing.

VALERE Rely on me. Three mouthfuls and you'll feel happily bloated.

HARPAGON That's it. And now, Jacques, it's time for you to go out and clean my carriage.

JACQUES Wait. You are now addressing your coachman. *(Puts on his overcoat.)* You were saying, monsieur?

HARPAGON Clean the carriage, groom my horses, and get ready to collect my fiancée.

JACQUES Your horses? They're not fit to walk, let alone drag a carriage. I won't say they're stretched out on their straw. The poor nags have none; it would be a sick joke. They get so little to eat that they're no more than phantoms in the shape of horses.

HARPAGON They're ill? When they do nothing?

JACQUES And because they do nothing, should they starve? It would be better for them to work a lot and eat heartily. I'm so fond of my old horses that I share my own meals with them. When I see them that thin and weak, it breaks my heart. It feels as if they're me. It's inhuman to have no compassion for a fellow mammal.

HARPAGON My fiancée lives just down the street, no distance.

JACQUES I haven't the heart to drive them. I'd feel guilty about cracking the whip. They might collapse in fright.

VALERE Leave it to me, monsieur. I'll persuade our neighbor to take charge of the horses.

JACQUES Good. I'd rather have someone else drive them to death.

VALERE The neighbor can also give us a hand with the reception.

HARPAGON Do we need him?

VALERE He'll do it out of friendship.

HARPAGON Are you sure?

VALERE Ab-so-lutely. He thinks the world of you.

JACQUES I can't stand flatterers, monsieur, and I can see what this
one's up to with all this taking over other people's jobs and cutting
down on the bread and wine, wood, salt and candles. All he wants is
to soften you up. That gets me indignant. It's bad enough when I hear
what people hereabouts say, because I'm sort of attached to you, yes I
am, in spite of everything. Next to my poor, dying horses, you're the
creature I like most.

HARPAGON People speak about me?

JACQUES If I tell you what they say, you'll take take it the wrong
way.

HARPAGON Not at all.

JACQUES Pardon me, monsieur, I know you'll lose your temper.

HARPAGON No, please. I'd be gratified to learn how others esteem
me.

JACQUES You asked for it. They tell stories about how you take a
bath once a year in cold water and stand up afterward till your dry so
as not to squander the water, and then you pour it back in your pond
for the horses and cattle to drink. And they laugh at the way you pick
fights with the servants just before Christmas and then fire them so
you won't have to pay them for the holiday. And I heard that a stray
cat nibbled some fat off a bone that had been thrown out, and you
took the scrawny beast to court for unarmed robbery. Then there was
the night when you crept out to the stable to snatch some of your
horses' oats for breakfast and your coachman, the one before me,
couldn't see who you were in the dark, and beat you up. Yes,
monsieur, it's a pity, but people grin as soon as anyone speaks your
name, and they start swapping tales about your ah, economical ways.
Sometimes they call you the vampire and sometimes the leech.

HARPAGON *(Beating him)* You're a brainsick good-for-nothing, money-for-everything liar, and a disloyal dog. *(Throws down his stick and leaves.)*

JACQUES *(Calling after him)* That's what I meant by your temper.

VALERE You see? Your honesty was the worst policy.

JACQUES Bootlicker! Laugh at your own beatings when you get them, not mine.

VALERE Now, now. Don't be upset.

JACQUES *(Aside)* He's backing off. I'll bear down on him. If he's scared, I may even thump him a couple. *(Aloud)* Me, I'm not in a laughing mood. Rub me the wrong way and I'll make you grin out of the other side of your big mouth. *(He pushes Valére across the room.)*

VALERE Whoa! Easy, easy!

JACQUES I'll block off your brown nose.

VALERE Please!

JACQUES Please won't help.

VALERE But —

JACQUES Where's that stick? I'll beat the bumps out of you.

VALERE Is this the stick you're looking for? *(He picks up the stick and pushes Jacques back across the room.)*

JACQUES No, not that one. I didn't mean a real stick.

VALERE You're a dismal, pathetic coward.

JACQUES Only when I'm in danger.

VALERE Nothing more than a damp slop of a cook-impersonator.

JACQUES It's what I do best.

VALERE You said something about beating the — what was it? bumps out of me?

JACQUES I was clowning.

VALERE *(Beating him)* You're — a — very — funny — clown! *(Exit.)*

JACQUES *(As he picks up the stick, bending with difficulty, and addresses it)* I'm not blaming you for what happened. *(He kicks the stick, thinks, kicks it again.)* You taught me a useful lesson. *(He kicks the stick again.)* Honesty is the worst policy. I must break myself of the habit. I don't mind a beating now and then from the old man. But this manager — *(Pretending to thrash Valère)* I'll — make — him — pay!

Enter Frosine with Mariane.

FROSINE Jacques, do you know if the master's at home?

JACQUES He is. I can feel it.

FROSINE Please tell him I'm here with his fiancée.

Exit Jacques.

MARIANE Oh, I dread this meeting.

FROSINE Why, girl? I'm here. What are you worried about?

MARIANE Picture a woman going to the gallows and waiting to see that instrument of death.

FROSINE I daresay Harpagon isn't the most beautiful way to die. But if I read your expression right, you're still thinking about that young man who visited your house.

MARIANE He was so ... polite.

FROSINE Did you discover who he is?

MARIANE No, but he was so... likable.

FROSINE Yes, these young society types are attractive enough, and they spin a charming line of talk. But most of 'em are as poor as mice. You're much better off making do with an old man who can set you up financially. You may not enjoy much in the way of a marital experience. You may even have to fight down your disgust. But once he's dead, you're in a position to accept somebody else, somebody young, who will make it all up to you.

MARIANE I don't want my happiness to depend on an old man's death.

FROSINE You do! Listen now: You marry him on condition that you swiftly become a widow. That has to be written into the contract. Then it'll be fraud if he survives for more than three months. Here he is, halfway through death's door.

MARIANE Oh, Frosine, what a horror!

Enter Harpagon, followed by Valère.

HARPAGON Don't be offended, my young beauty, if I come before you wearing glasses. I know that your charms leap before the eyes. I need no glasses to perceive them. But we look at the stars through lenses, and I insist that you are a star, a star that is the most dazzling star in the land of stars. *(Silence. To Frosine)* What's this? She doesn't greet me, and she shows no sign of pleasure.

FROSINE She's still stunned at capturing you. And then, very young women are bashful about revealing what's in their hearts.

HARPAGON I hope so. Here, lovely child, my daughter wishes to welcome you.

Enter Elise.

MARIANE Do forgive me for not calling on you sooner.

ELISE No, I should have called first on you.

HARPAGON *(To Elise)* Don't start a fight. *(To Mariane)* Look how big she is! Weeds grow fast. No wonder, with her appetite.

MARIANE *(To Frosine)* He's hateful.

HARPAGON   What did the little dolly darling say?

FROSINE   She finds you fascinating.

HARPAGON   You're too kind, you delicious creature.

MARIANE   *(To Frosine)*   He's a brute.

HARPAGON   Thank you, thank you, for those sweet sentiments.

MARIANE   *(To Frosine)*   I can't stand him!

HARPAGON   And here comes my son to pay *his* respects.

Enter Cléante.

MARIANE   Oh!   *(To Frosine)*   He's the one I told you about.

FROSINE   *(To Mariane)*   Oh lord, what an awkward coincidence!

HARPAGON   I see you're astonished that I have such grown-up
children. Don't worry: I'll soon sweep them out of the house.

CLEANTE   To be candid, madame, this is an event I couldn't
possibly have foreseen. My father told me of his plans only a few
hours ago.

MARIANE   This meeting is as much of a surprise, monsieur, to me
as to you. I wasn't prepared for it.

CLEANTE   My father couldn't have chosen better, madame. I'm
honored to meet you. But I can't assure you that I'm pleased at the
prospect of becoming your stepson. My congratulations stick in my
throat. I apologize, but stepmother is not a title I wish on you.
These remarks might seem coarse to some people, but I'm confident
that you know how to take them. This is a marriage I can't help
finding repugnant. Knowing who I am, you will understand how it
runs counter to my own interests. With all respect to my father, if I
had my way, this marriage would not take place.

HARPAGON   Take that back, every uncivil word, or I'll —

MARIANE   There's no need for that, monsieur. Your son's feelings
and mine correspond. *(To Cléante)* If you're repelled by seeing me

as your stepmother, I'm no less repelled by having you for a stepson. Please don't blame me. I'd be most put out if I caused you any displeasure. Unless I am forced into it by powers beyond my control, I give you my word that I will not consent to a marriage that distresses you.

HARPAGON   That told him back. I apologize, my dear, for his discourtesy. He doesn't weigh the consequences of his words.

MARIANE   No, I'm glad he speaks candidly. From him that confession was welcome. Now we both know where we stand.

HARPAGON   In time he may grow wiser. You'll see him change his mind.

CLEANTE   I could never change my mind. I hope the young lady will believe me.

HARPAGON   More inanity! He's as blatant as ever in his hatred.

CLEANTE   Do you want me to belie my feelings?

HARPAGON   And more yet! Can't you change the subject? Make some interesting conversation.

CLEANTE   Certainly. Since my father asks me to speak in a different vein, I'll put myself in his place. I've never seen any woman more appealing than you, madame, and I can think of nothing that would exceed the happiness of making you happy. You are worth more than all the kingdoms of history. You radiate a light I can only describe as celestial, and you'd make even the most impassioned and inventive compliments sound inadequate. For your sake I would —

HARPAGON   Steady there, my boy. You're overdoing it.

CLEANTE   I'm paying your felicitations to the lady.

HARPAGON   Good God, I can speak for myself.

CLEANTE   Of course you can, father, and I'm sure you will. Madame, have you ever seen a brighter diamond than the one on my father's finger?

MARIANE   It is brilliant.

CLEANTE   *(Taking it off Harpagon's hand and giving it to her)*   See it close up. Study it.

MARIANE   Oh!   It's alive with light.

She offers it back to Harpagon. Cléante steps in front of her.

CLEANTE   No, no!   It belongs on the hand it's in now. Take it as a gift from my father.

HARPAGON   *(To Cléante)*   From me?

CLEANTE   Don't you insist the lady keep it as a token of love?

HARPAGON   *(To Cléante)*   My diamond!

CLEANTE   Madame, he gave me a sign. You must accept it.

MARIANE   He's too impulsive. I couldn't.

CLEANTE   He refuses to take it back. Don't offer it.

HARPAGON   *(Aside)*   He'll drive me mad!

MARIANE   But —

CLEANTE   You'll only insult him.

MARIANE   Please!

CLEANTE   Impossible.

HARPAGON   *(Aside)*   I'll flog that thieving young —

CLEANTE   Now he's growing enraged at your reluctance.

HARPAGON   *(To Cléante)*   Highway robber!

CLEANTE   You see? He's losing his usual patience.

HARPAGON   *(To Cléante)*   Cut-throat!

CLEANTE   Don't blame me, father. I'm doing all I can to persuade her, but she's stubborn.

HARPAGON   *(To Cléante)*   Assassin!

CLEANTE   Madame, because of you my father's reproaching me.

HARPAGON   *(To Cléante)*   Back-stabber!   Father-killer!   Oedipus!

CLEANTE   Madame, you'll make him unwell.   Please don't resist any longer.

FROSINE   For heaven's sake!   All this to-do!   Keep the ring, if that's what he wishes.

MARIANE   *(To Harpagon)*   I'll keep it, so as not to offend you, but only for the time being.

Jacques enters in a rush and bowls Harpagon over.

JACQUES   Monsieur —

HARPAGON   He's killed me!

CLEANTE   Father, are you all right?

HARPAGON   He's taken bribes from my enemies to break my neck.

VALERE   I don't think you're damaged.

JACQUES   Sorry about that, monsieur.   I hurried in because there's a man here to see you.

HARPAGON   I'm busy.   Next week.

JACQUES   He's brought some money.

HARPAGON   I'm coming.   *(False exit.)*

CLEANTE   Oh, father, shall I order in lots of additional refreshments?   This is a big celebration.

HARPAGON   *(To Valère)*   Stop him, for God's sake, or he'll beggar me. And put aside as much food as you can ahead of time so that we get some money back from the merchant.

VALERE   Very good.

HARPAGON   *(Aside)*   Wicked, wicked son, you want me impoverished — in the gutter.   *(He smacks his forehead.)*   The man with the money!   *(Exit, running.)*

[THIS IS THE END OF ACT THREE.]

PART TWO

Mariane, Elise, Frosine, and Cléante, as before.

CLEANTE Now father's gone, we can talk openly.

ELISE My brother has confided in me, Mariane. I know he loves you, and I'm completely, affectionately on your side.

MARIANE Thank you, Elise. I hope I can always count on your friendship.

FROSINE You two should have warned me earlier that you're in love.

CLEANTE Mariane, how can we put a stop to this marriage?

MARIANE I'm a dependent and a minor. I can only hope for the best.

CLEANTE Hope? Is that all? No encouragement, no action, no enterprise?

MARIANE I leave them to you. Please don't ask me to break the contract.

CLEANTE Will you imprison me in the clauses of a contract?

MARIANE I can't go back on my mother's promise. But I'm willing to tell her about my feelings for you.

CLEANTE Frosine, dear and clever lady, can't you help us?

FROSINE With all my heart. I always had a soft spot for young lovers, and by nature I'm a giver, a doer.

ELISE Find some way to stop what you started.

FROSINE Not so easy. We can talk to your mother, Mariane.
Perhaps she'll transfer the gift of a bride from the father to the son.
But the stumbling block, as I see it, is Cléante's father. The
rejection must come from him. Mariane, we need to make him
unlove you. *(The others nod.)* Yes, that's *what* we have to do.
The big question is *how*. I'm thinking, I'm thinking, I'm thinking
furiously.

CLEANTE If you come up with an answer, I promise you the fattest
commission you ever collected.

FROSINE Money. That'll sharpen my thinking. I know someone
who might handle the money side.

CLEANTE Good. And Mariane, work on your mother. Don't stint
on the eloquence. Take ruthless advantage of her fondness for you.
Kiss her. Caress her.

MARIANE I'll do my best. Can we get away for a few minutes?

Re-enter Harpagon. He stops at the doorway.

HARPAGON *(Aside, tossing a coin)* Only one crown, but well
worth stepping outside for . . . What's going on here? My son
kisses the hand of his stepmother-to-be, and his stepmother-to-be
raises no strenuous objections. Is there some hanky-panky?

ELISE *(Warning them)* Here's father.

CLEANTE Father, we have a little time before dinner. Shall I escort
my stepmother on a tour of the house?

HARPAGON Your sister can do that. I need you here. *(Exeunt
Frosine, Elise, and Mariane.)* So . . . apart from your view of
her as a stepmother, how does my intended strike you?

CLEANTE Her personality?

HARPAGON Everything. Her bearing, her looks, her intelligence,
her manner.

CLEANTE I hardly noticed. Frankly, I felt disappointed. Her
manner is flirtatious, her bearing's rather clumsy, her looks are
mediocre, and her intelligence is pedestrian. But as I say, I wasn't

really observing her. Don't conclude that I'm trying to put you off, father. As stepmothers go, she's probably no worse than most.

HARPAGON But you did say to her —

CLEANTE Yes, a few polite words. To please you.

HARPAGON Then you yourself have no personal inclination there?

CLEANTE None.

HARPAGON That's a pity. I had an idea. Watching her here, I thought about my age and wondered what people would say to see me marrying a girl so young. I even considered withdrawing my proposal. But I made a formal promise to her mother. If you didn't dislike her, I'd give her to you.

CLEANTE To me?

HARPAGON You.

CLEANTE In marriage?

HARPAGON Marriage.

CLEANTE She's not my ideal, that's true. But I'll force myself to marry her, if that's your wish.

HARPAGON No, you can't have a good marriage where there's no inclination.

CLEANTE The inclination may come with time. They say love is often the fruit of marriage.

HARPAGON Too much of a risk from the man's side. It could prove disastrous. If only you'd shown some inclination ... But that wasn't to be, so I'll follow through with the original plan and marry her myself.

CLEANTE Well, father, if that's how it stands, I'll open my heart to you. The truth is: I've been in love with her since the first time I saw her. I meant to ask you this morning if I could marry her. What held me back was simply that you declared your love first, and I couldn't bring myself to upset you.

HARPAGON   Have you been to see her?

CLEANTE   Yes, father.

HARPAGON   Often?

CLEANTE   Often enough, in the time we had.

HARPAGON   Did she and her mother welcome you?

CLEANTE   Yes, but without knowing who I was. That's why
Mariane looked so surprised when she saw me.

HARPAGON   Did you say you loved her and wanted to marry her?

CLEANTE   Certainly. I even informed her mother.

HARPAGON   And she listened to the proposal?

CLEANTE   Yes, very courteously.

HARPAGON   And does the daughter return your love?

CLEANTE   If I can believe what I see and hear, father, I feel sure
she has some affection for me.

HARPAGON   Cléante my boy, you know what you must do now?

CLEANTE   Yes?

HARPAGON   Stop running after a girl I intend for myself. Marry the
rich widow fate has chosen for you.

CLEANTE   So this is how you toy with my feelings. Well, I tell you
now: I won't give up my love for Mariane. I'll fight for her. I'll go
to any lengths. You may have the mother's consent, but I have
other powers on my side.

HARPAGON   You dare to invade my territory?

CLEANTE   You invaded mine. I was there first.

HARPAGON   Am I or am I not your father?

CLEANTE   That's what I've been led to believe.

HARPAGON   Do you or don't you owe me respect?

CLEANTE   Love is no respecter of persons.

HARPAGON   I'll teach you who's a respecter with a thick stick.

CLEANTE   Your threats won't move me.

HARPAGON   You will give up Mariane.

CLEANTE   I will not.

HARPAGON   A stick here, ho!

Enter Jacques.

JACQUES   What's this?   Father and son at each other's throats?

HARPAGON   Talking to me in that tone!

CLEANTE   I won't budge one millimeter, so there!

JACQUES   That's no way to speak to your father.

HARPAGON   I'll pound some obedience into him with my stick.

JACQUES   That's no way to speak to your son. To me, fair enough, but —

HARPAGON   Jacques, in this dispute, I'll let you be the judge.

JACQUES   You will?   Marvelous!   I'll do it. *(To Cléante)* Step over there.

HARPAGON   There's a girl I want to marry. That spendthrift there has the gall to love her, in spite of my orders.

JACQUES   He's wrong.

HARPAGON   A son competing with his father!   Shouldn't he do his duty by me and withdraw when it comes to my inclination?

JACQUES   Let me have a word with him. Wait there. *(He crosses to Cléante.)*

CLEANTE   It doesn't matter to me who referees. I'm only too glad, Jacques, to tell you my side of the argument.

JACQUES   The privilege is mine.

CLEANTE   I'm in love with a young lady. She loves me in return. She accepts my offer of marriage. Then my father butts in by asking her to marry him.

JACQUES   He's wrong.

CLEANTE   Shouldn't he feel ashamed when he thinks of marrying again at his age? A girl? Is it becoming for him to fall in love? Shouldn't he leave love to young people?

JACQUES   He can't mean it. Let me have two words with him. *(Aside)* Farewell, honesty, forever! *(Returning to Harpagon)* Well, your son is not as obstinate as you make him out. He's ready to talk reason. He says he's aware of the respect he owes you; he's no longer carried away by that first excitement; and he won't hold out against anything you say, so long as you treat him with more consideration and give him a wife he can like.

HARPAGON   If that's so, tell him he can hope for everything he wants from me. Barring Mariane, I'll let him take any woman he chooses.

JACQUES   I'll report back to him. *(Crossing to Cléante)* Well, your father's not as obstinate as you make him out. He said it was your defiance that infuriated him. He'll grant you anything you wish, as long as you behave respectfully.

CLEANTE   Jacques, assure him that if he lets me have Mariane, I'll be the most obedient of sons. I'll never oppose his wishes.

JACQUES   *(Returning to Harpagon)* It's arranged. He agrees.

HARPAGON   Thank God!

JACQUES   *(Crossing to Cléante)* It's settled. He's satisfied.

CLEANTE   Couldn't be better.

JACQUES   Peace is restored. You two were at odds because of a mere misunderstanding.

CLEANTE   My dear man, I'll be grateful to you all my life.

JACQUES   You're welcome.

HARPAGON   Jacques, you've made me content. You deserve a reward. *(Reaches into his pocket. Jacques holds out his hand. Harpagon takes out a handkerchief. He dusts Jacques's lapel, shoulder, and hand.)* Go now. I'll remember this.

Jacques looks at his hand, turns it over, looks at the other hand, shrugs, and leaves.

CLEANTE   I apologize, father, for my inexcusable behavior.

HARPAGON   I'm delighted to find you so amenable.

CLEANTE   It's great-hearted of you to forgive my faults.

HARPAGON   That's easy to do when a son remembers his duty.

CLEANTE   And you no longer resent my extravagance?

HARPAGON   I can't when you promise to be respectful.

CLEANTE   I'll tell everyone about your generosity.

HARPAGON   You'll have reason to. You shall have whatever you ask for.

CLEANTE   I don't ask for anything more.

HARPAGON   My dear, dear, obedient boy!

They embrace.

CLEANTE   You see, you give me more than I could ever want when you give me Mariane.

HARPAGON   What was that?

CLEANTE   I said, I'm more than satisfied to have Mariane.

HARPAGON   Who said anything about letting you have Mariane?

CLEANTE   You did.

HARPAGON   I did? You promised to give her up.

CLEANTE   I did? I did not.

HARPAGON   You still claim her?

CLEANTE   Of course. More than ever.

HARPAGON   What, again? You two-faced backslider!

CLEANTE   Nothing can alter my resolve.

HARPAGON   I forbid you to see me again — ever!

CLEANTE   It won't be too soon.

HARPAGON   I disown you as my son. I disinherit you.

CLEANTE   Thank you. I'm free.

HARPAGON   *(Storming out)*   And I give you my curse.

CLEANTE   *(Calling after him)*   I don't want any of your gifts.

Enter La Flèche, carrying a cash box.

LA FLECHE   Master! I've found you just in time. Follow me!

CLEANTE   What's wrong now?

LA FLECHE   Nothing. We're in luck.

CLEANTE   How come?

LA FLECHE   This box — from the garden.

CLEANTE   What's in it?

LA FLECHE   Your father's gold. I dug it up.

CLEANTE   When? How?

LA FLECHE   I'll tell you everything. Let's run. I can hear him shouting.

Exeunt Cléante and La Flèche at high speed.

Enter Harpagon, at equally high speed, from the garden.

HARPAGON   Thieves, thieves, everywhere thieves! Justice, oh just heaven! I'm lost, I'm done for. They've stolen my money. Who did it? What's become of him? Where is he? Did he hide? Did he run? Run where? Or not run? Is he here? Isn't he there? Who is he? Stop! *(Grabbing his own arm)* Crook, give me back my money. No, it's me! I'm going mad. I don't know who I am, where I'm standing, if I'm standing, what I'm doing. Help, help! My poor money, my dear money, my sweetheart, they've taken you from me, my prop, my comfort, my only joy, my everything. Life's at an end. I have nothing left in this world. I don't want to live without my money. *(Sinking down)*   I'm drained, I'm dying, I'm dead, I'm buried. *(Sitting up)*   Won't someone revive me by giving me back my money? Or tell me who took it! What's that? What did you say? Nobody's there. The criminal picked the right time, waited till I was talking to my treacherous son. I must go — somewhere. I'll find a magistrate. I'll have everyone in the house searched — my servants, my son, my daughter, the horses . . . *(Noticing the audience)*   Who are these people? They look suspicious. All of them are the thief. What are they talking about over on that side? The murderer who robbed me? What's that whispering at the back? Is that my thief? For pity's sake, if you have any information . . . He's down there with you, isn't he? They're staring. They're starting to laugh at me. They're all in league with my thief. Hurry, you commissioners, men-at-arms., marshals, magistrates, instruments of torture, gallows, executioners! I'll hang the whole world, and then, if I don't get my money back, I'll hang myself. *(He is prostrate.)*

[THIS IS THE END OF ACT FOUR.)

Enter the Commissioner, holding a notebook, pen, and inkwell.

COMMISSIONER   A felonious commotion, hey?   Just what I like to handle.   I didn't start catching criminals this morning, thank the lord.   I'd like to have fifty thousand crowns for every criminal I've hanged.

HARPAGON   *(Weakly)*   Fifty thousand crowns?

COMMISSIONER   Yes, and I'm not talking about your petty slime and filth, the pilferers, poachers, moochers, and bandits.   I mean the big boys, the emperors of crime.   Rape, contraband, arson, larceny, multiple slayings — my specialties.   I do it all by brilliance.   I penetrate the corrupt mentality with the aid of ferocious questions, whips, chains, and hot pokers.

HARPAGON   *(Recovering)*   Bring in the whole judicial system.   If I don't regain my money I'll take the law itself to law.

COMMISSIONER   *(Writing)*   We must conform with the necessary legal procedures.   Your complaint?

HARPAGON   A gang of thieves — they stole my cash box.

COMMISSIONER   Very good.   *Very*   good.   And what did you have in this alleged cash box?

HARPAGON   What does anybody keep in a cash box?

COMMISSIONER   Ah, there you'd be surprised.   Recipes, love letters, diaries, secret codes, pressed flowers, cough medicine, and dead birds, mostly.

HARPAGON   Mine had fifty thousand crowns in it.

COMMISSIONER   Fifty thousand crowns?   Where did you get that much?

HARPAGON   If this theft goes unpunished, the most sacred treasures are no longer safe.   I demand the severest penalty.

COMMISSIONER   Do you suspect anybody?

HARPAGON Everybody. I want you to arrest the whole town. And the outlying counties.

COMMISSIONER We mustn't frighten the community. We proceed with tactical caution and gather the damning evidence. Then we zoom in on our target and prosecute with all desirable vigor.

Enter Jacques, calling offstage.

JACQUES I'll be there in a moment. Have them slit his throat for me, singe his feet, drop him in scalding water, and hang him from the ceiling.

HARPAGON Have you caught my thief?

JACQUES Your manager just sent me a sucking pig. I want to dress it for you in a flamboyant new sauce.

HARPAGON Forget about that. Speak to this policeman.

COMMISSIONER Commissioner.

JACQUES Is he taking part in the reception?

COMMISSIONER Don't be nervous, my dear fellow. We'll tackle this exciting business with judicious calm. I want you to remember that you must conceal nothing from your master.

JACQUES I'll be proud to show you my prowess at the stove.

HARPAGON We're discussing something else, idiot.

JACQUES If I don't create the most mouthwatering meal possible, blame your manager, who's been clipping my wings with his blunt scissors.

HARPAGON Forget about the reception for the time being. I want you to give me some particulars about my stolen money.

JACQUES You've had some money stolen?

HARPAGON Yes, you fog-headed fool, and I'll have your fatuous hide if you don't give it back.

COMMISSIONER   Please don't bully him. He has an honest face.

JACQUES   Don't I?

COMMISSIONER   If I'm mistaken, we can always toss him into a dungeon and work over his fingernails and other extremities. My friend, speak up and we won't even heat the irons, and you'll get a reward from your master.

JACQUES   Prove it.

COMMISSIONER   His cash box was lifted today. You must know something about it.

JACQUES   *(Aside)* This is my chance. That manager's been the favorite since he got here. No suggestions listened to except his. And that stick, that beating . . .

HARPAGON   What are you muttering?

COMMISSIONER   He's turning over the evidence in his mind. I told you he was honest.

JACQUES   You want the truth, monsieur?

COMMISSIONER   Nothing but.

JACQUES   I believe your manager took it.

HARPAGON   Valère? The man I trusted?

JACQUES   That's the one. I believe he did it because you trusted him.

HARPAGON   On what grounds do you believe it?

JACQUES   Grounds?

HARPAGON   Yes.

JACQUES   I believe it on the grounds that . . . I believe it.

COMMISSIONER   But you must produce your evidence.

HARPAGON   Did you see him prowling where I had my money?

JACQUES   Yes, I did. Where was your money?

HARPAGON   In the garden.

JACQUES   That's where I saw him. In the garden. Ab-so-lutely.
What did you have the money in?

HARPAGON   A cash box.

JACQUES   That was it. I saw him sitting on a cash box.

HARPAGON   What was the box like? We'll soon know if it was
mine.

JACQUES   What was it like? It was like . . . like a cash box.

COMMISSIONER   We're aware of that. Describe it.

JACQUES   It was a big box.

HARPAGON   Mine is small.

JACQUES   Yes, of course it was small, if you look at it that way. I
call it big because of what it had inside.

COMMISSIONER   What color was it?

JACQUES   The color?

COMMISSIONER   The color.

JACQUES   The color was a bright sort of . . . Give me a hint.

HARPAGON   You're not color-blind?

JACQUES   Not as a rule. Wasn't it . . . red?

HARPAGON   No, gray.

JACQUES   Certainly. Reddish-gray. That's what I meant.

HARPAGON No doubt about this: it's the one. Write it down, commissioner. Get his deposition. God, who is there to trust? From now on I wouldn't even trust myself.

JACQUES Here he comes now, slinking toward us. Just don't let him know I was the one who had the guts to report on his atrocities.

Enter Valère.

HARPAGON Come here. I hold you responsible for everything.

VALERE I hope so, monsieur. And I'm proud to be.

HARPAGON What! You don't even blush?

VALERE For what?

COMMISSIONER The grandest larceny yet perpetrated on these premises.

HARPAGON Your vile deed, monster. Your crime!

VALERE My what? Oh yes, I see what you're getting at.

HARPAGON It's all out in the open now. I've been apprised of the entire sickening story. How could you abuse my kindness and insinuate yourself into my home to betray me? I never heard of such a sordid deception.

VALERE Since you know everything, I won't attempt any denial.

JACQUES *(Aside)* God above, did I guess right?

VALERE I meant to take up the matter with you. I was waiting for a suitable opportunity. But now we've reached this point, I ask you not to be angry. Please listen to my reasons.

HARPAGON And what fine reasons can you give, you charlatan, you impostor, you thief?

VALERE It's not fair to call me a thief. I've committed an offense against you, yes, but it's a fault you can forgive.

HARPAGON Forgive! An ambush, a devastation like that?

VALERE   When you hear me out, you'll realize it's not as bad as you think.

HARPAGON   Not as bad!   When you've taken my blood, my vitals?

VALERE   Your blood hasn't fallen into evil hands. My rank will ennoble it. And I will make amends.

HARPAGON   So you shall. You'll restore what you took from me — and in perfect condition.

VALERE   Your honor shall be fully satisfied.

HARPAGON   It's not a question of honor. Tell me, what made you do such a thing?

VALERE   Must you ask?

HARPAGON   Yes, I must.

VALERE   A god who has excuses for all his mischief. Love.

HARPAGON   Love, he says. Love, by God! Love of my gold coins.

VALERE   Your wealth didn't tempt me. I have no design on what belongs to you, so long as you let me keep the one thing I took.

HARPAGON   By every devil in and out of hell, I will not. Look at this for impudence: He wants to keep what he stole from me!

VALERE   You call it stealing?

HARPAGON   What else? A treasure like that.

VALERE   A treasure, true enough, your dearest resource. But if you let me keep it, you won't lose it.

HARPAGON   Now he has the nerve to try and strike a bargain.

VALERE   We promised, my treasure and I, to love one another. We took an oath never to be parted.

HARPAGON   I smile at the oath and laugh at the promise.

VALERE Yes, we swore to remain together forever.

HARPAGON Your "forever" is already coming to an end.

VALERE Only death can separate us.

HARPAGON It probably will if my money has taken that much of a hold on you.

VALERE I've already said that it wasn't greed that drove me to do what I did. I'm not as heartless as you suggest. I was moved by a loftier emotion.

HARPAGON Next he'll be wanting my money out of Christian charity. But the law will settle accounts for me, you bare-faced, scheming, teeming liar.

VALERE I can face any reasonable punishment, because I am the only one to blame. Your daughter's not at fault.

HARPAGON I should hope not. I want to get back what's mine without further delay. Where did you carry it off to?

VALERE I didn't carry anything off. Your treasure is still in your house.

HARPAGON *(Aside)* Oh, my own cherished box! *(Aloud)* Not out of the house, you say?

VALERE Of course not.

HARPAGON But did you try to . . . open anything up?

VALERE Could I dream of doing such a thing? My love burns with a pure flame.

HARPAGON *(Aside)* He burns for my cash box!

VALERE I'd sooner perish than give way to one questionable thought about a soul so chaste.

HARPAGON *(Aside)* My cash box with a soul that's chaste!

VALERE I allowed myself to look. I couldn't restrain myself. But I could never take advantage of the passion in those lovely eyes.

HARPAGON *(Aside)* She has a lock. She has two beautiful compartments. But lovely eyes?

VALERE Your housemaid knows the truth, and she can verify that we —

HARPAGON So — enlisting my servant as an accomplice?

COMMISSIONER This is growing serious: an accessory before the fact, abetting and subornation.

VALERE She knows my intentions were beyond reproach.

HARPAGON Is it fear of the law that makes you rave?

VALERE I'm saying that I had a difficult time before my love could triumph over her modesty.

HARPAGON Whose modesty?

VALERE Your daughter's. She wouldn't commit herself to signing the marriage agreement until yesterday.

HARPAGON Elise signed a marriage agreement?

VALERE With me. Yes.

HARPAGON Oh dark skies, storms, tidal waves, earthquakes!

JACQUES Write it down, commissioner, write. Earthquakes.

HARPAGON Yes, hurry, commissioner. Do your duty and draw me up his indictment for being a thief *and* a seducer.

VALERE These are unjust accusations. When it becomes known who I am—

Enter Elise, Mariane, and Frosine.

HARPAGON You spiteful child! Daughter unworthy of a father like me! You let yourself fall in love with an infamous thief. Worse, you signed a marriage agreement with him. But you'll earn your rewards, both of you. *(To Elise)* For you, four thick convent walls. *(To Valère)* For you, the noose.

VALERE   Before I'm condemned, I'll at least be heard.

HARPAGON   I was wrong to say noose. I'll have you broken on the wheel.

ELISE   *(Kneeling)*   Father, I implore you, show a little humanity. Give yourself time to think. Look closely at this young man. He's not remotely what you take him for. Without him, you'd have lost me. Yes, he was the one who saved me when I was in terrifying danger, close to drowning. You owe him my life.

HARPAGON   I'd be much better off if he'd let you go under, instead of doing what he's done since.

ELISE   Father, in the name of your love for me —

HARPAGON   What love? What name? I don't want to hear. The law must take its course.

JACQUES   *(Aside)*   He'll pay for that beating.

FROSINE   *(Aside)*   What a shambles! We'll never straighten it out. Unless . . .

Enter Anselme.

ANSELME   Is something wrong, Harpagon? You look agitated.

HARPAGON   Ah, Count Anselme, I'm the unluckiest man alive. We've run into so much grief over your marriage contract. My parenthood! My honor! My resources! This scoundrel sneaked into my house as a servant to deprive me of my money and deprave my daughter.

VALERE   What is this money you keep blustering about?

HARPAGON   They signed a marriage agreement. This is an affront to you, Count Anselme, and you ought to be the one to take action. Lodge your complaints against him to the full expense — I mean, extent — of the law.

ANSELME I don't intend to marry anyone by force. But when it comes to your interests, I'll uphold them as if they were mine.

HARPAGON Commissioner, press the formal charges. Make them fierce and make them stick. Spare no cost, and give the bill to my friend the count. He's the injured party.

VALERE I don't see what crime you can manufacture out of my love for your daughter. As for punishment, when it becomes known who I am —

HARPAGON Who you are! I'm sick of all these charades. The world's overflowing with down-and-outs who give themselves titles and degrees and rich parents and the first illustrious connections that spring into their swollen heads.

VALERE I don't need any false credits. Everybody in the city of Naples can testify to my birth.

ANSELME Watch what you say. You're taking a bigger risk than you imagine. You're speaking in front of a man who's familiar with Naples and may easily see through your story.

VALERE I have nothing to be ashamed of. If you know Naples, you have heard of Don Thomas d'Alburcy.

ANSELME I have. Few people know him better.

HARPAGON I don't give a damn for Don Thomas or Don Jackass.

ANSELME Let him speak. We'll hear what he has to say about d'Alburcy.

VALERE I say that he was my father.

ANSELME You call yourself the son of Don Thomas d'Alburcy? Then let me point out that more than sixteen years ago the man you speak of escaped with his wife and children from the brutalities that followed the uprising in Naples. At that time many noble families fled into exile. Don Thomas, his wife, son, and daughter died at sea.

VALERE Not quite. The son of Don Thomas, aged seven, and a servant, were dragged from the wreckage by the crew of a Spanish galleon. The captain raised the boy, me, as his son. He trained me to handle a sword, musket, and pistol. Not long ago I learned that my father had not died. In searching for him, I came ashore near here and, by chance, the first person I met was this lovely young woman, Elise. I fell madly in love with her and resolved to stay near her by serving in her father's household, while I sent my servant Pedro to continue looking for my family.

ANSELME   Have you any proofs?

VALERE   Yes. Here: this bracelet from my mother and this seal with an inset ruby from my father. And my old servant Pedro, when he returns.

MARIANE   You're not an impostor. Everything you said makes it plain that you're my brother. My mother has often enthralled me by telling the tale of how our vessel turned over and splintered. Heaven preserved us both from death, but only because we were captured by pirates. They kept us in slavery for ten years before letting us go. We returned to Naples, but we found all our property sold. My mother's relatives sneered at us because we were now poor. We fled from them, living from hand to mouth in different parts of Europe. Eventually we were glad to take refuge here. And at last I am reunited with my only brother.

ANSELME   Embrace me, my children!

VALERE   You are our father? Alive?

MARIANE   Mother has so often wept for you.

ANSELME   Yes, my daughter. Yes, my son. My true name is Don Thomas d'Alburcy. Like you, I was saved from the storm and the wreck with my fortune intact, praise heaven. I went back to Naples to sell off my belongings. Then I searched all over Europe for you. Finally I settled here in the hope that changing my name and surroundings might make my long grief easier to bear. But the loneliness oppressed me. I could not get over the loss of my loved ones. I thought I might start a new family by marrying this young lady. Now it appears I've found my family. And she has found the man she wants to marry. And so have you, my daughter. Let us all kneel and thank the Almighty for our incredible victory over time and suffering.

HARPAGON   One moment. This man is your son?

ANSELME   He is.

HARPAGON   I hold you responsible for paying back the fifty thousand crowns he stole from me.

ANSELME   My son robbed you?

HARPAGON   Nobody else.

VALERE   Who told you that?

HARPAGON   Jacques.

JACQUES   As you can see, I'm saying nothing.

VALERE   Monsieur, do you think me capable of such an act?

HARPAGON   Capable or not capable, I want my money back.

Re-enter, with exquisite timing, Cléante and La Flèche.

CLEANTE   Don't torment yourself, father. I have good news for you. If you let me marry Mariane, your money will be returned.

HARPAGON   Where is it?

CLEANTE   I know where it is. Now, your decision: Either give me Mariane or say good-by to your cash box.

HARPAGON   Has anything been taken out?

CLEANTE   Not one thing. Make up your mind: Are you going to let us marry? Her mother has given Mariane permission to choose between us.

MARIANE   Cléante, there's something you don't know yet. My mother's consent is no longer enough. God has given me back my father and brother. You must ask them for my hand.

ANSELME   I haven't found you, my children, in order to oppose your vows. Harpagon, you must know that a girl will always pick the son over the father.   Come now, don't compel me to say what you don't need to hear.   Consent to this double marriage, as I do.

HARPAGON   Before I form an opinion, I must see my cash box.

CLEANTE   You'll see it, safe and intact.

HARPAGON   I have no money to give my children.

ANSELME   I have.

HARPAGON   Will you pay for both weddings?

ANSELME   I will.   Are you satisfied?

HARPAGON   Not yet.   Will you pay for my wedding suit?

ANSELME   Don't you have one?

HARPAGON   I rented it to a friend.

ANSELME   One wedding suit.   And now, at last, let's celebrate this supremely joyful day.

COMMISSIONER   Wait.   Not so fast, please.   *(Waving his notebook)*   Who defrays the expenses for my official documents?

HARPAGON   To us your documents are nothing.

COMMISSIONER   Perhaps so, but I don't draw them up for nothing.

HARPAGON   *(Pointing to Jacques)*   For payment I'll give you this man to add to your collection of hangings.

JACQUES   What is morality?   They beat me for telling the truth and now they'll hang me for lying.

ANSELME   Harpagon!   Forgive him.

HARPAGON   You'll pay the commissioner, then?

ANSELME   I will.   That must be the last obstacle.   *(Everybody cheers.)*   Let's hurry, children, to meet your mother and share the happy tidings.

HARPAGON   I don't forgive anybody or anything until I see my cash box.

Rejoicing, drinks, festivity.

La Flèche brings in the cash box. Harpagon snatches it from him. While the others are celebrating, he stands cradling it in his arms and crooning to it, alone.

THE END

Lyrics for **The Miser**

"Sad Love."
Duet: Valère and Elise.
Insert on page 47 to replace the first four speeches of the play.

VALERE	Elise!
ELISE	Valère?
VALERE	Elise, be fair.

You're hiding something:
I see a trace
of sadness in that lovable face.
You sigh —
but why?
You look as if you're ready to cry —
be stronger!
I'll love you till the second I die —
or longer.
Tell me what's the matter, please,
my sweet Elise.

ELISE	Valère!
VALERE	Elise?
ELISE	Valère, don't tease.

I thought of something
and felt downcast:
I've often heard that love doesn't last.
You men
know when
to make a pretty speech to a girl,
bewitch her,
to put her head and heart in a whirl
then ditch her.
That's the matter. Do you care,
my dear Valère?

Continue with Valère's line on page 47: "Don't judge me by others,"
etc.

Reprise of "Sad Love."
Duet: Cléante and Elise.
Insert on page 48 after Cléante's entrance.

CLEANTE	Elise!
ELISE	Cléante?
CLEANTE	Elise, I want
	to whisper to you,
	although offhand
	I'm sure you never can understand.
	You're cool,
	no fool.
	You wouldn't have a clue how it feels —
	now would you? —
	to fall for someone head over heels —
	how could you?
	That's my secret, my disease,
	sister Elise.

Continue with Elise's line at bottom of page 48: "You're in love?"

"Fifty Thousand Crowns."
Solo: Harpagon.
Insert on page 53 after Harpagon's line: "Don't go through the garden!"

HARPAGON

> Oh, happy is the man without suspicion
> who has his nest-egg nicely in position
> for earning dividends, and keeps in play
> only the sums he needs from day to day.
> But me, I aggravate myself, I chafe.
> The unsafest place for money is a safe.
> It actually attracts your average crook:
> a safe's the first place where he goes to look. . .
>
> How I puzzled!
> How I cudgeled
> till I nearly wrecked my brains
> to find a quiet spot to stash
> a quite inordinate lump of cash

and hide it from the thieving trash
my family entertains.

Now yesterday I took in a commission
plus capital: my loan to a physician,
a buy in real estate. We both came off it,
I don't mind saying, with a noble profit
in coinage, not commodities or stocks.
But where the devil could I put the box?
The bed? no, bad. The outhouse? (Beg your pardon.)
I planted it at midnight in the garden . . .

Fifty thousand!
Fifty thousand!
Fifty thousand crowns all told!
I tossed all night; I wept in doubt.
Suppose some stray dog roots 'em out?
Or gardeners digging thereabout?
It makes my blood run hot and cold.
Fifty thousand francs in gold!

*Continue dialogue near the end of Harpagon's long speech: "What
did I say?"*

"You're Right."
Duet: Valère and Harpagon.
*Insert on page 59, after Valère's line. "No, but you couldn't
be wrong."*

HARPAGON

I'm giving her a mate,
a man no more than fifty.
He's wealthy and sedate
and best of all he's thrifty.
But then this wicked hussy
turns quarrelsome and fussy.
She's spoiling for a fight.
Which one of us is right?

VALERE

You're right, you're right, you're right!
She hasn't seen the light.

(Speaking) On the other hand, she's not altogether
mistaken, because —

HARPAGON

You'd think she might be glad,
not squabble, and disparage
a man who never had
a child from his first marriage:
no daughter and no sonny
between her and his money!
You don't need second sight
to see that I am right.

VALERE

You're right, you're right, you're right.
This man is dynamite.

(Speaking) Still, perhaps she feels you're rushing things a bit and
she needs time to —

HARPAGON

You'll never hear him make
proposals that are flowery.
But listen now: he'll take
this wench without a dowry!

VALERE *(Speaking)* No dowry?

HARPAGON *(Speaking)* Not a sou.

VALERE *(Speaking)* That's the most impressive argument yet. All
the same, you might want to consider —

HARPAGON

The saving is tremendous.
His social rank will send us
Up to the loftiest height.
Which one of us is right?

VALERE

You're right, you're right, you're right!
Your logic's watertight.

HARPAGON

The wedding is tonight.

Continue with Valère's lines near the top of page 60: "Still, your daughter might claim that marriage is a serious commitment," etc.

Reprise of "You're Right."
Solo: Harpagon.   Insert on page 61 after Valère escorts Elise out.

HARPAGON
> That boy's a loyal, fervent,
> and dedicated servant,
> an oracle *and* polite,
> my worthy proselyte.
> I picked him out of spite:
> I'm bright, I'm bright, I'm bright!

Continue with entrance of Cléante and La Flèche on page 62.

"Sound of the Contract."
Solo: La Flèche.
Insert on page 63 after La Flèche's line: "You'll have to sign this."

LA FLECHE
> Privacy, property, family, notary, security. . .
> Lá-la, la lá la.
> Solidity, sincerity, prosperity, equity, maturity . . .
> Lá-la, la lá.
> As long as we observe
> the absolute formality
> this document shall serve
> with fine-drawn finality,
> and brevity, amity, courtesy, tranquillity,
> euphony, unity — any possibility.
> Lá-la, la lá,
> lá-la, la lá,
> lá-la-la, lá-la-la, lá-la-la, ha ha!

CLEANTE   *(Speaking)*   And if something goes wrong?

LA FLECHE   *(Speaking)*   They've provided for that too:
(Singing)   Adversity or perfidy,
> discovery, mendacity,
> mean usury, penalty, poverty, catastrophe. . .
> Lá-la, la-lá, la-lá, ha ha!

Continue on page 63 with Cléante's line: "Nothing to quarrel with so far."

"So Young."
Solo: Frosine.
Insert on page 68 after Harpagon's line: "Yes, what is it, Frosine?"

FROSINE

> You've grown so young
> you must have done it by stealth.
> Stick out your tongue.
> Good God, it's blazing with health!
> I'd say you've sprung
> from some perennial stock.
> Puff up that lung.
> It feels as hard as a rock . . .
>
> You have a mark between your eyes
> that means you'll live to beyond five score,
> and on your hand you can see this line
> that reads One-Twenty, maybe more. . .
>
> Put you among
> the toughest men of our time.
> They'll come unstrung
> to find you still in your prime.
> I've never sung
> a more solemn truth:
> You, my friend, have recaptured your youth!

Continue with Harpagon's line on page 68: "Is that possible?"

Reprise of "So Young."
Solo: Frosine.
Insert on page 71 between Frosine's words, "No, no!" and "Let me see you walk."

FROSINE

> You've grown mature,
> the mellow, sensible type.
> As your amour,
> she wants a partner who's ripe.
> You can be sure

how secure she'll feel:
You, my sage, are an age-old ideal.

"They Like You."
Solo: Jacques.
Insert near the bottom of page 78 afterJacques's line: "You asked for it."

JACQUES

They like you so much they tell hundreds of jokes about
how you take once-a-year cold-water soaks and stand in the
tub till you're dry, not to squander the water, and then pour it
back in your pond for the horses and cattle to drink. And
they blast you for printing up calendars where every fast is
extended from one day to three, so your staff goes hungry or
munches on grass. And they laugh at the way you pick
fights with your servants and hit them unmercifully and
compel them to quit before they've been paid. And I hear
that a cat that belonged to your neighbor and nibbled some
fat off a bone in the garbage was taken to court for stealing.
And then there's a comic report of the night when you crept
out and entered the stable to eat the stale fodder your horses
weren't able to swallow, and your driver, the one before me,
caught you there in the dark and exacted a fee with his stick
for the fodder. Monsieur, it's a shame but they break up
when anyone mentions your name. They mock your apparel,
your movements, your speech, and they call you the
vampire, or sometimes the leech.

Continue with Harpagon's beating him and saying, "You're a brainsick," etc, on page 78.

"Look on Me Kindly."
Solo: Harpagon.
Insert on page 81 after Harpagon's entrance.

HARPAGON

Look on me kindly,
fairest maiden,

> if I come before you
> with glasses on my eyes. . .
> They're not to remind me
> through sight that's fading
> of the charms and more you
> immortalize.
> But we look at the stars through lenses,
> and I insist that you are
> of all the stars in the land of stars
> the most dazzling star.
> So listen to me kindly
> and let me be him for whom
> you shed light across the firmament
> of this room.

MARIANE *(Speaking, aside)* This tomb.

Continue on page 81 with Harpagon's words to Frosine: "What's this?," etc.

"Step Relations."
Duet: Cléante and Mariane.
Insert on page 82 after Harpagon's "I'll soon sweep them out of the house."

CLEANTE

> I dare not swear I'm overjoyed
> to welcome you, madame,
> in such a role. You fill a void,
> I guess. I shouldn't feel annoyed.
> My father wants you as his bride.
> I put my troubled thoughts aside
> and say to you: If you can,
> go ahead and marry the man.
>
> Stepmother is a word I dislike,
> Stepson, a title I disown:
> Two steps that jar,
> two steps too far.
> They make me sound like a tyke
> and you a crone.
> That's why I dare not swear I'm overjoyed
> to welcome you, madame.

HARPAGON *(Speaking)* Some congratulations!

MARIANE

> When everything is said and done,
> I'm not dismayed, monsieur.
> If I'd been forced to take a son,
> before you I'd choose anyone.
> I'd love to break our present ties
> and know you in some other guise.
> And so I say that the plan
> is for me to marry the man.
>
> Stepson's an epithet I abhor,
> Stepmother — ugh! — that I detest.
> Two steps awry
> and this is why:
> They make you sound like a boor
> and me a pest.
> Therefore, when everything is bought and paid,
> I'm not dismayed, monsieur.

Continue on page 83 with Harpagon's "That told him back," etc.

Reprise of "Step Relations."
Solo: Cléante.
Insert on page 83 after Cléante's ". . . I'll put myself in his place,"
etc.

CLEANTE

> I'd cast away all rights of birth
> to marry you, madame.
> I count you as of higher worth
> than all the kingdoms of this earth.
> You radiate celestial light.
> You make all compliments sound trite,
> and so I mean, as a man,
> to be yours as soon as I can —

Continue with Harpagon's "Steady there, my boy," etc, on page 83.

"We'll Hook Him."
Frosine, with chorus (Elise, Cléante, Mariane).

Insert on page 88, after Frosine's last words: "...I'm thinking furiously."

FROSINE

>We'll hook him, we'll hook him,
>we'll well and truly cook him.
>We'll pop him when he's hot
>in the marriage pot.
>
>All we need's a stylish, gallant
>lady with my kind of talent.
>Have her play a viscomtesse
>or a foreign-born princess.
>Dress her up in slinky gowns,
>say she's worth X million crowns.
>All her castles swarm with vassals
>wearing gold and silver tassels,
>jewels, and the rest of it.
>Trust me to make the best of it.

CHORUS

>We'll hook him, we'll hook him,
>we'll well and truly cook him.
>We'll pop him when he's hot
>in the marriage pot.

FROSINE

>Let your father hear us talking.
>Make his ears start somersaulting
>when he learns that she's aflame
>for his person and his name,
>thinks his stinginess maligned,
>worships his dogmatic mind,
>loves the way he ties his breeches,
>wants to hand him all her riches,
>jewels, and the rest of it.
>Trust me to make the best of it.

CHORUS

>We'll hook him, we'll hook him,
>we'll well and truly cook him.
>We'll pop that poppa in the marriage hopper

before he knows where or what . . .
We'll plot him into the matrimonial pot.

Continue with Cléante, top of page 88: "If you come up with an answer," etc.

Reprise of "We'll Hook Him."
Solo: Commissioner.
Insert on page 96, after the Commissioner says: "Just what I like to handle."

COMMISSIONER

I'll hook him, I'll hook him,
I'll well and truly book him.
I'd like to have a grand
for every rogue I've hanged.

It's a fact: I always landed
villains, felons, single-handed.
Not your small-time filth and slime.
Big boys, emperors of crime!
How? By doggedness, resilience?
No, I do it all by brilliance,
worm my way inside their brains
with the aid of whips and chains,
hot pokers, and the rest of it.
Trust me to make the best of it.

I'll hook him, I'll hook him,
I'll well and truly book him.
For arson and for larceny,
for rape and contraband,
for all the pilferers, poachers, moochers —
all the scum I've canned —
I should have been awarded some very high command.
And I'd like to own
a precious stone
for every rogue I've hanged.

Continue with Harpagon on page 96: "Bring in the whole judicial system."

"Tale of a Separation."
Three solos: Valère, Mariane, Anselme.
Insert on page 105, after Valère's words: "Not quite."

VALERE

> The son of Don Thomas, aged seven,
> and a servant were dragged from the wreck
> by the crew of a tall Spanish galleon
> whose captain took them on his deck.
> I swear it's the truth.
> I have all the proof.
> I swear, if you care, it's the truth

> He treated me like his own offspring.
> He trained me to master a sword,
> as well as the crew of a galleon,
> and assured me that I'd be restored
> to my parents. I came ashore near here
> and, by chance, the first person I met
> was my lovely Elise in the briny,
> looking quite irresistibly wet.

> I swear it's the truth.
> I have all the proof.
> I swear, yes I dare, it's the truth.

> I'll attest to my birth: See this bracelet
> from mother, this seal d'Alburcy
> from father — and please question Pedro,
> the servant who was rescued with me

> I swear it's the truth.
> I have all the proof.
> I swear that I'm sharing the truth.

MARIANE *(Speaking)* You're not an imposter. Everything you told us makes it plain that you're my brother.

> *(Singing)*
> My mother has often enthralled me
> with our tale of disaster at sea.
> As the vessel turned over and splintered
> she clung to a spar — and to me.

> I swear it's the truth.

I have all the proof.
I swear, though it's rare, it's the truth.

Gracious heaven preserved us from drowning,
but pirates then took us in tow.
They kept us for ten years in slavery
and worse — before letting us go.

We boarded a vessel for Naples,
where we found all our property sold.
My mother's own brothers despised her,
so we fled to the north and the cold.

I swear it's the truth.
I have all the proof.
I'll swear anywhere it's the truth.

Through Europe we wandered and suffered.
We knew that we had to survive
in order to be reunited,
and here I am, poor but alive.

I swear it's the truth.
I have all the proof.
I swear and declare it's the truth.

ANSELME   *(Speaking)*   Embrace me, my children!

VALERE   *(Speaking)*   You are our father?

MARIANE   *(Speaking)*   For whom mother has so often wept.

ANSELME   *(Speaking)*   Yes, my daughter.   Yes, my son.
           (Singing)
My name is Don Thomas d'Alburcy.
Like you, I was saved from the main,
with my fortune intact, praise to heaven,
and I sought you all over in vain.

I swear it's the truth.
I have all the proof.
I swear it's the square, honest truth.

I sold my Italian belongings

and settled here in the belief
that changing my name and location
might help to allay my long grief.
But loneliness seized and oppressed me.
I felt unattached and unwhole,
and thought I might start a new family
by marrying this gentle, young soul.
Now I, it appears, have my loved ones,
while she, it appears, has a swain.
Let us all kneel and thank the Almighty
for our loss and incredible gain.

They all kneel, except Harpagon.

CHORUS

It has to be true.
It's long overdue:
The actual, miraculous truth!

Continue on page 107 with Harpagon's line: " This man is your son?"

Reprise of "So Young."
Solo: Frosine.
Insert on the middle of page 108, after Harpagon's words: "Not yet."

FROSINE

You've grown so mean
that it's no longer a joke —
so full of spleen
you'd watch a dying man croak.
You're a cold-fisted, tight-wristed, old, twisted money-
machine.
I mean it: mean!

Continue on page 108 with the rest of Harpagon's line: "Will you pay ," etc.

"Reunion."
The cast.
Insert on page 108, after Anselme's words: "I will."

MARIANE
> I have my brother again.

VALERE
> I'll see my mother again.

HARPAGON
> And I'll get my cash box back.

ANSELME
> I'll need no other again.

CLEANTE and ELISE
> I've won my lover again.

HARPAGON
> And I'll get my cash box back.
> I miss my cash box.
> Life *is* my cash box.
> Can't wait to kiss my cash box
> when she comes back.

JACQUES and FROSINE
> In joy they'll smother again.

COMMISSIONER and LA FLECHE
> We'll all recover, and then

HARPAGON
> Then I'm set
> to face any threat,
> cover any debt,
> never again fret,
> do a pirouette
> or a minuet
> after I get
> my pet of a cash box
> back in my arms —
> my more than adorable cash box back!

*This can serve as the finale, or lead into the stage directions
suggested for the end of the play on page 109.*

POSTSCRIPT

Another translation of *The Miser?* By now the play is a classic outside France, as well as at home, and has weathered many English renderings, some of them broadly adapted, others transliterated almost word for word. (The tastiest one, composed by Baker and Miller in the1730s, survived as an authentic antique in the Everyman series until a few years ago.)

The version presented here came into being as a script for contemporary directors and actors; that much is implied by the title of this first of three books. It is aimed squarely at the theatre, and yes, it is faithful, and no, it is not faithful.

It is faithful in that it derives from a literal translation I started with and retains the original sequence of scenes and speeches. The names and the settings and the coinages remain French, and I strongly advise against Americanizing them, for practical and not merely dogmatic reasons. Any directors who try to force the play into an immigrant mold and mode will confront their actors with beliefs and attitudes that are wildly out of kilter with those of contemporary Americans. If they imagine our audiences will not buy foreign names and currency, they have not reckoned with the volume and enthusiasm of our 20th-century touring innocents who go abroad, a striking proportion of them to France.

It is unfaithful because several of the servants are omitted and their lines put into the mouth of La Flèche in the opening and closing scenes of Act 3; because the Commissioner's Clerk has gone; because I have cut the scene breaks, which mark entrances and sometimes exits and seem unnecessary today. One item from the dialogue has also been cut: Frosine's intention, stated but never fulfilled, to recruit a woman "of my talent" to impersonate a rich and titled lady who will seduce Harpagon away from his attraction to Mariane. This text is shorter and less formal than Molière's, but in line, I hope, with his desire to find a speech that sounds fairly natural in the theatre. Finally, I have added some bits of verbal embroidery.

To justify this last distortion — which is most blatant in the lines of the Commissioner — I must plead not only translator's poetic license but also commercial avarice. This is an age of piracy, like every other age. Directors and literary advisers habitually, almost routinely, cobble together versions of Ibsen, Chekhov, Molière, Strindberg, and other plain-speaking playwrights that they find in and out of the public domain, a sentence from here, a phrase from there. As a weak sort of protection, I have tried to establish a copyright *within* the text by making the lines distinctive and therefore recognizable as theft, if they appear elsewhere. This is a gesture rather like that of Georges Méliès who sneaked proprietary claims onto the frames of his films; they were subliminal, invisible, as the frames rolled forward, to the naked eye or even to what Perelman once called the well-dressed eye, but in the event of piracy — which happened often — Méliès or his agents could identify the films as unmistakably his. However, I choose to put a rosy, artistic complexion on these additions and think of them as hand-detailing.

Directors who wish to depart even further from Molière can make use of the lyrics appended at the end of the play, and can secure or write music for them. They replace some swatches of dialogue and occasionally call for new linking lines, which are provided. Frosine's plan to impersonate a titled lady is restored in these lyrics — which can, of course, be recited as narration, rather than sung.

As for *George Dandin,* this is more or less a straightforward translation. No other English version of the play remains in print as of this writing; the last one was published by Stark Young some sixty years ago and appeared in a poetry magazine that is difficult to find except in specialized libraries, from some of which it has inevitably vanished. ·A tragifarce of the first rank and as such a precursor of much recent drama, *Dandin* needs reintroducing, and is included here, as a public service, with no adornment.

For aid and goading that overflow the boundaries of acknowledgment I warmly and fraternally thank: Ron Moody, Peter Coe, Leo Shapiro, M. Abbott Van Nostrand, Lawrence Harbison, Helen Merrill, Glenn Young, an array of actors who would have delighted Molière; Joyce, Neil, and Derek Bermel, and twenty years of colleagues and students.

Albert Bermel
The Bronx, New York, 1987